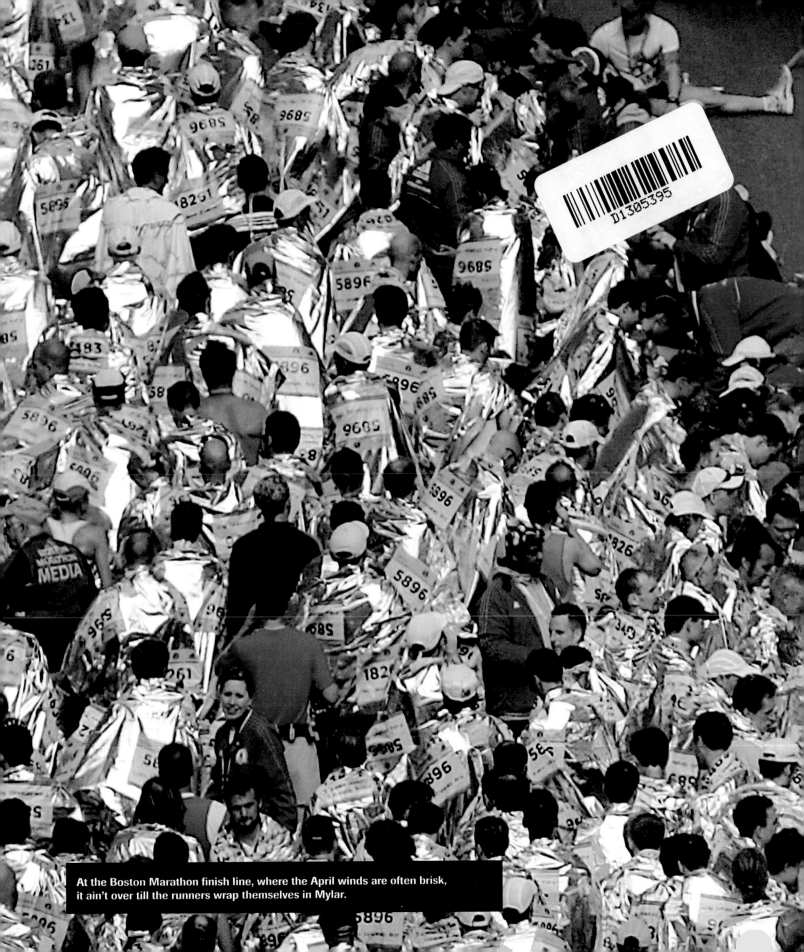

At the Boston Marathon finish line, where the April winds are often brisk, it ain't over till the runners wrap themselves in Mylar.

This book is available in quantity at special discounts for your group or organization. For further information, contact:

Triumph Books
542 S. Dearborn Street
Suite 750
Chicago, Illinois 60605
Phone: (312) 939-3330
Fax: (312) 663-3557

Printed in U.S.A.
ISBN 13: 978-1-57243-892-7
ISBN 10: 1-57243-892-4

EDITOR: JANICE PAGE
ART DIRECTOR/DESIGNER: WENDY DABCOVICH
ASSISTANT EDITOR: JIM COFFMAN
RESEARCHER AND MVP: BEN CAFARDO
PHOTO IMAGER: ERIC NORDBERG
ARCHIVE EXPERT: LISA TUITE

WRITERS:

Michael J. Bailey, Jack Barry, Ron Borges, Joe Burris, Ben Cafardo, Nick Cafardo, Marc Carig, Robert Carroll, Tony Chamberlain, Jim Coffman, Bud Collins, Joe Concannon, Frank Dell'Apa, Bob Duffy, Kevin Paul Dupont, Gordon Edes, Bella English, Ken Fratus, Peter Gammons, Stan Grossfeld, Judy Van Handle, Bob Hohler, Michael Holley, Adam Kilgore, Jackie MacMullan, Michael Madden, Steve Marantz, Nancy L. Marrapese, Barbara Matson, Peter May, Jim McCabe, Bob Monahan, Leigh Montville, Jerry Nason, Andy Nesbitt, Janice Page, Marvin Pave, John Powers, Hillary Read, Bob Ryan, Dan Shaughnessy, Fluto Shinzawa, Michael Smith, Chris Snow, Scott Thurston, Michael Vega

PHOTOGRAPHERS:

John Blanding, 124, 125, 132, 141, 158; John Bohn, 19, 25, 91; Antoine Bolanger/ Pawtucket Red Sox, 86; Bill Brett, 103, 105, 107; Jerry Buckley, 109; Barry Chin, 18, 25, 61, 82, 83, 90, 122, 123, 131, 146, 147, 157; Jim Davis, 5, 14-17, 20, 22, 24, 42-45, 47, 49, 62, 69, 88, 89, 96, 97, 113, 118, 119, 121; Bob Dean, 54; Ted Dully, 10; Danny Goshtigian, 39; Bill Greene, 21, 46; Stan Grossfeld, 23, 63, 75, 77, 93, 114, 115, 128; Tom Herde, 38; Ellis Herwig, 36; Heinz Kluetmeier/ Sports Illustrated, 27; Matthew J. Lee, 112, 152; Paul J. Maguire, 85; Frank O'Brien, 30, 33-35 37, 40, 51-53, 64, 65, 69, 76, 78, 79, 81, 100, 127, 135-137, 151; Joanne Rathe, 73, 106; Evan Richman, 6, 19; George Rizer, 95, 141; David L. Ryan, 2, 56, 134; John Tlumacki, 48, 128; Lane Turner, 121; Marc Wilson, 130

Additional photos courtesy of: Boston Globe archives, 57, 84, 104, 105, 116, 120, 135, 145; AP/Wide World Photos, cover shot of David Ortiz, 28, 66, 68, 70, 92, 99, 129, 142; Francis Ouimet Scholarship Fund, 149; Harvard Athletic Communications, 101

With special thanks to: Gregory H. Lee Jr. and the Boston Globe sports department, Globe photo and design departments, the Pawtucket Red Sox, Harvard Athletic Communications, Francis Ouimet Scholarship Fund

The Boston Globe

Not Till the Fat Lady Sings

BOSTON'S MOST DRAMATIC SPORTS FINISHES

Foreword by DOUG FLUTIE • Introduction by DAN SHAUGHNESSY

For many years, a "Reverse Curve" sign posted on downtown Boston's Storrow Drive got annual makeovers from vandals, who changed the sign to read "Reverse The Curse."

10 to start

40 more thrillers

After the 1984 Miami miracle, Doug Flutie had a street sign named in his honor at the Natick Mall.

The final moments of a tight game can be thrilling to relive. Still, I didn't think my Hail Mary pass to Gerard Phelan would be remembered as one of the greatest moments in college football history. I did think it would be something my teammates and I would all remember for the rest of our lives. Looking back on my college career, I want people to remember the things we did at Boston College and that I won the Heisman Trophy — not necessarily The Pass in Miami. But the legend of coming from behind with only 28 seconds on the clock lives on.

Obviously, that play was a big deal to us. By the time we got home to Boston, there were thousands of people at the airport and they were making such a big deal about it. Then all of a sudden you realize, "You know what, this was national TV, it was Thanksgiving weekend." I think all that added to the fact that it was a great game. That's what has made it as big as it has been.

The essence of a big play when you're behind is what goes on in your head right then and there. At that moment, I knew we had to make a big play to win the game. We had done it successfully before, so I didn't think it was impossible.

We all knew it was going to be the last play of the game, so we knew what the play call was going to be. They sent one of the young guys onto the field. I kind of waved him off because I wanted to leave Troy Stradford on the field. I didn't know Troy had a pulled hamstring at the time. But Troy stayed on the field anyway and we lined up. When we went to snap the ball the first time, there was a whistle and a flag and then they ended up picking up the flag. As we realigned for the second time, the guy that was on Gerard decided: "I'm going to walk over and get on [another player] instead," which allowed Gerard to get open and to be the first one down the field.

Basically you drop back, hang on to the ball for as long as you can, and throw it. But I always liked to scramble off to the right and get a little closer to the throw. The offensive tackle obviously didn't know this, so I almost got sacked getting around the corner. I wanted to peek backside at the tight end down the backside boundary, but I didn't have time (someone was running at me), so I just let it fly in the direction of the end zone. Not specifically to anyone, just in that direction.

I saw a big pile go up. The ball went over two defenders' heads and I just saw everybody fall to the ground and I assumed it was incomplete. There was probably a half-second delay to a second delay before I saw an official's arms go up in the back of the end zone. I was kind of chuckling to myself and running toward the pile.

Lots of gridiron miracles have happened since that fantastic moment in 1984, and heroes have come and gone. Thanks to Gerard, the Eagles, and the fans who can't forget a great play (and it truly was), I have something that people can identify with me. Two, three years after you retire, you're forgotten. At least that's something people will remember and have remembered for years.

The one big thing people didn't know is that the Heisman voting was basically in by then anyway. That pass did not win me the Heisman. I think (former Heisman winner) Joe Bellino said at that time that I had pretty much already won anyway.

Though the trophy's certainly a treasure, a spectacular, game-winning play in the clutch is what makes fans return to the stadium. That's what makes football great — and all of sports, for that matter: hoping to see a miracle. ... And sometimes the right decision at the right time can make it happen. This book is about those decisions and those moments and the other miracles that keep fans coming to Boston sports events of every stripe.

— *Doug Flutie*

INTRODUCTION

*I*t is the unexpected finish, the final-second reversal of fortune that separates sports events from other forms of performance art and entertainment. No matter how boffo a given theater company's production may be, we know that Hamlet is going to die at the end of the play. The Boston Pops can make hearts beat fast when they play the "1812" Overture on the Fourth of July, but no surprise accompanies that stirring sequence of sound.

Sports are different. We go to a game, watch TV, or maybe listen to the radio with our head on a pillow and we never truly know how an athletic contest is going to end. The thrill of victory can dissolve into the agony of defeat in a New York Minute — which is considerably more time than was needed for Aaron Boone to crush New England's spirit when he homered off Tim Wakefield in the 11th inning of the seventh game of the 2003 American League Championship series at Yankee Stadium.

Babe Ruth, Ted Williams, Rocky Marciano, Bob Cousy, Bill Russell, Bobby Orr, Larry Bird, Roger Clemens, and Tom Brady all began their careers in Greater Boston and light from these stars has illuminated the local sports landscape for almost a full century. But it is specific moments and plays, more than individual greatness, that is most deeply etched in our consciousness. On these pages we pay homage to Boston sports stories destined to live on in retellings long after participants and eyewitnesses are gone.

The selection process was the hardest part. What to include? What to leave on the cutting room floor? It's like choosing the best Beatles songs. A collection of Boston's most dramatic sports finishes could have been more voluminous than the Manhattan phone book, weighing perhaps as much as Doug Flutie. We have done our best to cover both the obvious and the not-so-obvious in this unranked list of more than 50 thrillers. Now, let the arguments begin.

Growing up in Central Massachusetts, hitting grade school just about the time Teddy Ballgame was handing the torch to young Carl Yastrzemski, I have been fortunate to witness a good number of the events in this book. I was in the first grade when the Patriots were invented (1960) and it wasn't until my freshman year of high school that I learned that our Celtics did not win the NBA Championship automatically every spring. That was the spring of 1967, which was also the beginning of the Red Sox Impossible Dream season, a six-month hardball campaign that forever changed the fortunes of New England's favorite team.

A career in sportswriting — more than a quarter century with the Globe — put me on the scene for many of these fantastic finishes, but no professional experience will surpass that night in St. Louis when the Sox put an end to 86 years of frustration. Like most Bostonians who consider baseball box scores one of the four major food groups, the story of the 2004 Red Sox ranks No. 1 on my list and is unlikely to be surpassed in my lifetime. October 27, 2004, was a night when the planets were aligned (literally, if you count the lunar eclipse), and I was there.

I was also there the night they shut down old Foxboro Stadium, a moment frozen in time like a real-life snow globe as Patriots kicker Adam Vinatieri drilled an icy football 45 yards through the uprights to put the oft-ridiculed Pats on a path to the first of their three (so far) Super Bowl championships.

My seat on press row at the old Garden put me close enough to practically touch Larry Bird when he inbounded the basketball during the 1984 NBA seven-game final victory over the Magic Johnson/Kareem Abdul-Jabbar Lakers. And from upstairs in the old barn, I got goose bumps whenever the Bruins crowd would drown out the final 30 seconds of the national anthem before another playoff game against the Canadiens.

There was never a fat lady on the ice for those anthems. That's how we knew it was never over. There's always a possibility of a storybook ending. That's what makes this book delightfully incomplete. There are more dramatic finishes in our future. It's the reason we watch the games.

— *Dan Shaughnessy*

10 to start

THE GREATEST COMEBACK EVER

Just like that, they shocked the nation.
Just as they pictured it, they changed the course of baseball history. And just like a dream, they dashed generations of heartache for New Englanders who longed to witness the one glorious triumph they staged in the October chill by the Harlem River.

In the greatest postseason comeback since the birth of the national pastime, the Red Sox completed a magical surge from a 3-0 deficit in the best-of-seven American League Championship Series by stomping the home-team Yankees, 10-3, in a do-or-die seventh game to capture their first pennant since 1986.

"How many times can you honestly say you have a chance to shock the world?" Kevin Millar said in the frothy celebration after the sensational finish. "It might happen once in your life or it may never happen. But we had that chance, and we did it. It's an amazing storybook."

Thanks to Derek Lowe's magnificent start and a big-bang attack led by Johnny Damon, series MVP David Ortiz, and Mark Bellhorn, the Sox became the first team in baseball history to come back from a 3-0 deficit to win a best-of-seven series. Four straight nights the champagne chilled in the Yankee clubhouse, and four straight nights the Sox dodged elimination, marking the first time in 14 years a Boston team beat the Pinstripers four times in as many days.

"How can this not be one of the greatest comebacks in the history of sports?" Sox principal owner John W. Henry said. "This team loves each other so much. They want to win so badly for one another and they wanted to win so badly for these fans. There's no way you can do this unless you have incredible heart."

Right: When the final out of the series was made in New York, the Red Sox bench (including Curt Schilling, Kevin Millar, David McCarty, and Derek Lowe) simply exploded.
Far right: David Ortiz knew the way home, and his walkoff blast in Game 4 spelled the beginning of the end for the Yankees.

Baseball

WHO	**RED SOX** VS **YANKEES.**
WHERE	**FENWAY PARK** & YANKEE STADIUM.
WHEN	**FOUR PERFECT DAYS** IN OCTOBER, 2004.
WHY THE DRAMA	No major league team had ever survived a 3-0 deficit, until this.

GAME 1 / OCTOBER 12	R	H	E
RED SOX	7	10	0
YANKEES	10	14	0

GAME 2 / OCTOBER 13	R	H	E
RED SOX	1	5	0
YANKEES	3	7	0

GAME 3 / OCTOBER 16	R	H	E
YANKEES	19	22	1
RED SOX	8	15	0

GAME 4 / OCTOBER 17	R	H	E
YANKEES	4	12	1
RED SOX	6	8	0

GAME 5 / OCTOBER 18	R	H	E
YANKEES	4	12	1
RED SOX	5	13	1

GAME 6, OCTOBER 19	R	H	E
RED SOX	4	11	0
YANKEES	2	6	0

GAME 7 / OCTOBER 20	R	H	E
RED SOX	10	13	0
YANKEES	3	5	1

Above: Ortiz had reason to jump for joy, and teammates were eager to join him at home plate.
Above right: Winning this pennant, against all odds, may have been the sweetest victory of all.

The Sox won the franchise's 11th AL pennant in a wondrous twist in a journey that began 243 days earlier when they gathered for spring training to avenge last year's heartbreaking loss in Game 7 of the ALCS to the Yankees. But they also scored sweet revenge for forebears such as Johnny Pesky and Bobby Doerr, who lost the final two games of the 1949 season to the Yankees with the pennant on the line, and Jim Rice and Dwight Evans,

who watched Bucky "Bleeping" Dent's home run ruin their chances for a division title in a one-game division playoff in 1978.

"There have been so many great Red Sox teams and players who would have tasted World Series champagne if it wasn't for the Yankees," general manager Theo Epstein said. "Guys in '49, '78, and us last year. Now that we've won, this is for them."

A preschooler in 1978, Lowe looked like an ace in the biggest start of his career to date as he whipsawed the Yankees over six innings, allowing only one run on one hit (RBI single by Derek Jeter), a walk, and a hit batsman. In so doing he completed his personal comeback from exiled starter when the playoffs opened to team savior.

While Lowe all but silenced a Yankee juggernaut that exploded for 19 runs in humiliating the Sox in Game 3, Damon staged his own remarkable reversal of fortune. He entered the game batting .103 with one RBI in the first six games of the series. But against right-hander Javier Vazquez, Damon launched a grand slam in the second inning and a two-run shot in the fourth.

This Game 7 marked the fifth time the Sox and Yankees put everything on the line on a decisive day of baseball, with one team keeping alive hopes for a World Series championship, and the other heading home empty-handed and heavyhearted. For the first time since 1904, it was the Red Sox who came through. ❖

MIRACLE WORKERS

OCTOBER 31, 2004 ▶▶ BY JOHN POWERS, GLOBE STAFF

They were deader than the Bambino, down three games to none to New York in the American League Championship Series after the worst playoff defeat in franchise history. Thousands of their fans had walked out on them in disgust. Four days later, the resurgent Red Sox had won their first pennant in 18 years with the greatest comeback in baseball history, beating their pinstriped tormentors inside the House That Ruth Built.

"Last year, we had a bad memory, and I saw a lot of my teammates destroyed," said David Ortiz, who so memorably kept his mates alive with two game-winning hits in the same calendar day, covering the ends of games 4 and 5.

The 11th-inning loss in Game 7 of the 2003 series was still fresh when the Sox arrived in the Bronx for the opener, with the New York tabloids eager to remind the visitors that the Yankees were their daddies. "Father's Day," proclaimed the Daily News.

When New York battered sore-ankled Curt Schilling and took an 8-0 lead amid six perfect innings from Mike Mussina, it seemed that nothing had changed since the previous October. But when Boston stormed back to within 8-7 before falling, 10-7, the Yankees sensed they'd be in for a grinder.

Boston had come from two games down to win Division Series against

Cleveland in 1999 and Oakland in 2003 and the Championship Series against Anaheim in 1986. But after dropping Game 2 by a 3-1 count on John Olerud's two-run homer off Pedro Martinez and Game 3 by a dispiriting 19-8, the Sox seemed threadbare beyond repair.

"To get destroyed like this when it's crunch time and have a football score up there at the end of the game, it's definitely embarrassing," said pitcher Bronson Arroyo, who gave up six runs in the first two innings plus.

Yet the Sox redeemed themselves by coming off the floor and producing consecutive extra-inning victories that seemed impossible in the wake of their

Left: **Big Papi, world champion.** Above: **Jason Varitek, Keith Foulke, and Doug Mientkiewicz made a very happy threesome after the final out in St. Louis.**

Finally, World Champs

After the Red Sox waited until the last possible instant to win the ALCS, they took command right from the start of the 2004 World Series. A thrilling 11-9 Game 1 victory that turned on a late-inning, bases-loaded situation set the stage for an eventual sweep.

Cardinals reliever Ray King put it best: "After the first game, when we had the bases loaded in a tie game and Scottie [Rolen] up, and we don't score, that was a major letdown right there."

Rolen popped up and the next batter, Jim Edmonds, took a third strike from Red Sox closer Keith Foulke. Then Mark Bellhorn hit a home run off the Pesky Pole in the bottom of the inning, and the Sox were on their way.

Three games and one lunar eclipse later, the curse was history.

GAME 1 / OCTOBER 23	R	H	E
CARDINALS	9	11	1
RED SOX	11	13	4

GAME 2 / OCTOBER 24	R	H	E
CARDINALS	2	5	0
RED SOX	6	8	4

GAME 3 / OCTOBER 26	R	H	E
RED SOX	4	9	0
CARDINALS	1	4	0

GAME 4 / OCTOBER 27	R	H	E
RED SOX	3	9	0
CARDINALS	0	4	0

Game 3 flogging.

First, the Yankees took a 4-3 lead into the ninth, but then Rivera walked leadoff man Kevin Millar and pinch-runner Dave Roberts and Bill Mueller went to work. Eventually Ortiz ("Who's Your Papi?") finished the 6-4 victory with a walkoff homer off Paul Quantrill in the 12th.

That was merely a prelude to the next night, when Boston rallied from two runs down in the eighth to win, 5-4, in the 14th, as six relievers held New York scoreless for the final eight innings.

"I might be in sort of a haze," conceded Sox general manager Theo Epstein, after Ortiz, who'd homered off Tom Gordon to lead off the eighth,

had knocked in Johnny Damon with the winning run. "But I think that was one of the greatest games ever played, if not the greatest."

Still, the Sox needed to win twice in New York, with one pitcher hurling on a stitched-together ankle and another whose previous Stadium outing had been a disaster. But when Schilling held the Yankees to one run in seven innings in Game 6. Mark Bellhorn bashed his three-run opposite-field homer for a 4-2 triumph and then Derek Lowe and Damon led the way in the 10-3 Game 7 victory, anything didn't just seem possible, it was. ❖

Right: **Sox fans rejoiced at a bar near Fenway.**

SUPER DRIVE

*T*here were 81 ticks of the clock, the Patriots were 83 yards from the end zone and there were no time outs left, on either side of the ball, in a tie game.

In the Fox-TV booth, John Madden weighed the circumstances and told a nation that prudence was the only proper course for the New England Patriots, and they were wrong to believe otherwise. Sit on the ball, run out the clock on the St. Louis Rams, take your chances in overtime.

But a different consensus already had been reached on the Patriots sideline, where Tom Brady, the quarterback, Charlie Weis, the offensive coordinator, and Bill Belichick, the head coach, huddled in the din of 72,000 fans still agog at the lightning speed (21 seconds!) in which the Rams had struck for the tying touchdown. The Patriots had come too far, stuck together through too much, prevailed in the face of peril too many other times not to take their chances one more time.

"Obviously," Weis would say later, "we could have kneeled on it and gone into overtime because neither one of us had any time outs, but we just felt that they had too much momentum and that we should at least give our starters a chance to win. Not play to lose, but play to win."

Thus was born what New England football fans will forever remember as The Drive, every bit as much as Denver Broncos fans reminisce about John Elway's 98-yard march down the field in frozen Cleveland to beat the Browns in the 1986 AFC Championship game, and as often as San Francisco 49ers fans recall Joe Montana guiding the Niners for 80 yards and a game-winning strike to John Taylor with 34 seconds left to beat the Cincinnati Bengals in Super Bowl XXIII.

"We'd done this before," guard Mike Compton said. "We knew we could do this again."

Brady's drive, unlike those of Elway and Montana, did not produce a touchdown. It culminated in something even bigger: the first championship in the 42-year history of the franchise, Adam Vinatieri's 48-yard field goal splitting the uprights as the clock read 0:00, the first Super Bowl to be decided by a kick on the final play.

Right: Out of the hold of Ken Walter, Adam Vinatieri booted the dramatic field goal that clinched the Pats' improbable Super Bowl win.
Far right: Tom Brady was showered in confetti and praise after leading his team to victory over the Rams in New Orleans.

Football

SUPER BOWL XXXVI

WHO	**PATRIOTS** VS **RAMS.**
WHERE	**LOUISIANA SUPERDOME,** NEW ORLEANS.
WHEN	**FEBRUARY 3, 2002.**
WHY THE DRAMA	New England had several chances to put the game away early in the second half. But who wanted another Super Bowl blowout?

A very Brady beginning

He had already shown he could lead his team to the playoffs, and he had proven he was a postseason winner before injury forced him to the sideline in the AFC championship game. But could young Tom Brady, a sixth-round draft choice just two years prior, lead his team to pro football's promised land with the score tied and the two-minute warning a distant memory?

He most certainly could.

In 2002, the 24-year-old signal caller became the youngest quarterback to lead his team to Super Bowl glory, capping off the first chapter of a legendary football story that within four years would include three thrilling championships.

Above: Torry Holt of the St. Louis Rams felt the squeeze from Tebucky Jones (left) and Teddy Bruschi of the New England Patriots during the first quarter of Super Bowl XXXVI.

Earlier, the Patriots had dominated the 14-point favorite Rams for three quarters, taking a 17-3 lead that could have been 24-3 if a Tebucky Jones 97-yard-fumble return touchdown hadn't been nullified by penalty. But St. Louis rallied in the fourth. They managed to tie the game, which set the stage for The Drive.

It began with Drew Bledsoe, the best quarterback in Patriots franchise history, but one reduced to offstage prompter by injury and Brady's magic. He pulled Brady aside just before the 24-year-old strapped on his helmet and trotted back onto the field. "Drop back and sling it," Bledsoe told the man who would become the youngest quarterback to be named Super Bowl MVP. "Go win the game."

Sling it he did, though always under control, just as he'd been throughout a mistake-free evening in which the Patriots played 60 minutes without a turnover. Seven times Brady passed, connecting five times, before he spiked the ball with seven seconds left at the Rams' 30, bringing the field

goal unit onto the field.

The first three completions were to running back Antowain Smith's understudy, J.R. Redmond, the English major from Arizona State who hadn't caught a pass all game in limited action. A little dump toss for 5 yards, and 24 ticks off the clock. Another short flick for 8 yards and a first down at the Patriots' 30. Forty-one seconds. After Brady spikes the ball to stop the clock, he goes back again to Redmond, who is able to fight his way out of bounds for a first down

after an 11-yard gain at the 41.

"I thought that was a big play on the drive," Belichick would say the next day. "J.R.'s catch, and he got it out of bounds. That's when we talked about wanting to get to the St. Louis 40 and have a shot at the field goal."

There were 33 seconds left, then 29 after Brady threw incomplete on first down. In the huddle, he called the play sent in from the sideline: 64-Max All End.

"Max tells the offensive linemen that we need more time," said Brady.

Above: Patriots wide receiver David Patten went airborne to pull down a second-quarter touchdown pass from Tom Brady at the Superdome.

"I dropped back, the offensive line did a heck of a job protecting me, and all three receivers ran routes at different depths.

One receiver in particular, Brady favorite Troy Brown, flashed free across the heart of the Rams' secondary.

"I stepped to the left and Troy, who has just got a great knack for finding the open zone, slipped behind there, and I hit him just coming out the back end," said Brady. "They missed the tackle and he got out of bounds.

"So it was just Troy making another great play. I can't tell you how many times I've seen him catch that type of pass and make guys miss like he did."

There were 21 seconds left after the 23-yard gain, the longest pass play of the night for the Patriots. The line of scrimmage was the Rams' 36. If the drive ended there, Vinatieri would be faced with a 53-yard field goal attempt; he'd been kicking them 55 yards before the game, and making them.

But there was time for one more pass play, a 6-yard dumpoff to the tight end in the red shoes, Jermaine Wiggins, the kid from East Boston. It took 14 seconds off the clock, but the 6-yard gain put the ball on the Rams' 30.

Seven seconds left. Vinatieri trotted onto the field. On the sideline, a team that had displayed its solidarity by running en masse onto the field at the start of the game now stood united once more, teammates holding hands and whispering silent prayers.

The snap and hold were perfect and the kick, well, Vinatieri said it best: "Once I kicked it, it was time to celebrate."

Right after the game, Patriots owner Bob Kraft accepted the Vince Lombardi Trophy from commissioner Paul Tagliabue and said, "The fans of New England have been waiting 42 years. We are the world champions. At this time in our country, we are all Patriots, and tonight the Patriots are champions." ❖

Clutch? Vinatieri had to have ice in his veins to make this game-saving kick against Oakland.

SUPER KICK

NOVEMBER 17, 2002 ❯❯ BY MICHAEL SMITH, GLOBE STAFF

Let's all agree for a moment that history follows a linear path. Now contemplate a few "ifs" regarding what is considered by several professional placekicking experts to be the most clutch field goal in NFL history: Adam Vinatieri's memorable fourth-quarter boot against the Oakland Raiders in the AFC divisional playoff on Jan. 19, 2002, at Foxboro Stadium.

What if, in the midst of the snowstorm and 25-degree temperatures, the fifth-most accurate among the hundreds who have attempted field goals in this league had gone against his usual routine and taken time during a 25-second eternity to take in the situation — and frozen with anxiety?

What if one of Vinatieri's linemen had committed a false start or held one of the Raiders, making it a 50- or even 55-yard attempt? What if long snapper Lonie Paxton had put too much or too little spin on the ball and spiraled it into holder Ken Walter's hands with the laces at 3 o'clock instead of 12?

What if Walter had mishandled the snap or failed to place the ball properly? What if Vinatieri momentarily had forgotten his fundamentals and attacked the ball, planted aggressively with his left foot, and tried for elevation rather than approaching it with caution and focus on simply making solid contact?

What if the prayers of an entire organization, the vast majority of 60,292 on-site witnesses, and thousands more watching on television and listening on radio had not been answered?

Here's what: Had Vinatieri's 45-yarder to tie the game with 27 seconds remaining not been good, life for New England sports fans, and the Patriots themselves, would be a heck of a lot less good.

For one thing, "We wouldn't have big rings," Vinatieri said. For another, "I wouldn't have a smile on my face every day like I do now," Paxton said.

There would have been no overtime to the game that quickly came to be known as the Snow Bowl, thus no 23-yard winner by Vinatieri, and no 16-13 Patriots victory. Walt Coleman still would be an anonymous referee and there would have been no ongoing controversy or conspiracy theories regarding the "tuck rule." Coleman ruled Brady hadn't quite tucked the ball away after his second-half pump fake, making his ensuing bobble an incompletion rather than the critical fumble the Raiders recovered.

There would have been no upset of the Pittsburgh Steelers by the Patriots the next week. In our alternate universe, the St. Louis Rams might be the game's latest dynasty, having won a second Super Bowl in three years.

Few occurrences in sports have meant as much to the fortunes of so many as Vinatieri's 135-foot drive in the final pro football game at Foxboro Stadium.

"The best one I've ever seen," Belichick marveled last week. "I saw [Tom] Dempsey's 63-yarder, but for everything — we can talk about that all day — but for everything that it was for, I would put it No. 1."

"I would have to agree with that," said Minnesota Vikings kicker Gary Anderson, a veteran of 21 seasons and the game's all-time leading scorer.

Before Vinatieri's decisive kick against the Rams in Super Bowl XXXVI, one other kicker, former Baltimore Colt Jim O'Brien, had won a Super Bowl in the game's final moments. O'Brien was a rookie when he drilled a 32-yarder against the Dallas Cowboys to win Super Bowl V, 16-13. In his estimation, his Super Bowl winner ranks third among the best pressure kicks in history, behind Vinatieri's snow kick and the championship clincher over St. Louis.

"Once he made that [kick against Oakland], I knew he could kick anything, anywhere, anytime," said O'Brien. The way he sees it, the 45-yarder in the snow "was the pinnacle of pressure kicks." ❖

Above: The young quarterback was definitely fired up over a fourth-quarter touchdown.
Below: Patriots defensive end Bobby Hamilton took an extra moment to frolic in the snow when the game was done.

MIRACLE IN MIAMI: THE PASS

It was the day after Thanksgiving, 1984. Little Doug Flutie and little Boston College were playing big bad Miami in a storied stadium known as the Orange Bowl.

Down 45-41, BC was 48 yards away from pay dirt with the final seconds ticking off the clock. Flutie rolled to his right and let it fly. It was the old "everybody go long" play. The ball sailed through the Florida sky and came down into the arms of Gerard Phelan, whose end-zone grab ushered it into history.

Life changed for Doug Flutie after The Pass. He was Bill Buckner in reverse. He was Mike Eruzione with a future in pro sports. He was a gifted local performer who forever will be associated with one play, one defining moment when he made all of our dreams come true.

"The assignment was basically to drop back and just let it fly and hang it up," said Flutie, who capped off what eventually became a 10-win season for BC by winning the Heisman Trophy. "For me, in that situation, I always tried to hang on to the ball as long as I (could) to allow everybody to get down the field. What ended up happening, in order to do that, I kind of scrambled out to the right and rolled right.

"I thought I was going to get drilled. I wound up and launched it. I saw the ball go down over two defenders' heads and I thought it fell incomplete into the end zone. And there was like a second [before] I saw the officials' arms in the back of the end zone go up. I didn't know who caught it. I started smiling and laughing to myself a little bit and then started running and jumping."

People always want to ask Willie Mays about his catch of Vic Wertz's fly ball in the 1954 World Series. Bobby Thomson talked and talked about his homer off Ralph Branca. Flutie's play is The Pass. Forever.

"I think it's the one signature play and the thing that people most remember me by," he said. "In a negative aspect, it's the only thing people remember about me. We had so many great games — winning the Heisman and all that other stuff.

"From my standpoint, I'd like people to remember those things. It almost gives me the impression that people think I was a one-play wonder and that was the only thing I ever did. So that's a little frustrating. But in general, it's given people something to remember me by and it's something that's kind of a trademark of my career."

How does he rank The Pass with The Kick — David Gordon's game-ending field goal to beat No. 1-ranked Notre Dame in 1993?

"I think David's field goal is just as important," Flutie said. "The Pass was more dramatic only because it was more improbable. But Dave's field goal was just as significant, especially to the program and their situation [at the time]."

Flutie's Hail Mary is put on a special pedestal perhaps because it was the golden play in what was at that time the golden age of Boston sports. In leading BC to its 10-2 mark that year, he passed for close to 3,500 yards and 27 touchdowns. In the Miami game, Flutie had compiled 421 passing yards before the Hail Mary was even launched, and the epic back-and-forth duel with Bernie Kosar's Hurricanes would have been a worthy classic even if BC had lost.

Right: Doug Flutie got a big lift from his brother, Darren Flutie, after the Hail Mary pass had landed.

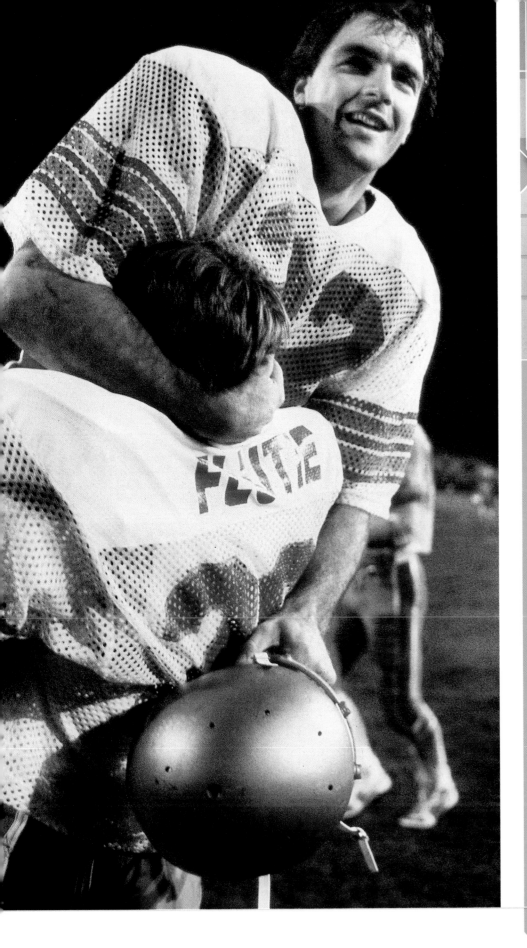

College

FOOTBALL / REGULAR SEASON GAME

WHO	**BOSTON COLLEGE** VS. **UNIVERSITY OF MIAMI.**
WHERE	**ORANGE BOWL,** MIAMI.
WHEN	**NOVEMBER 23, 1984.**
WHY THE DRAMA	This game's dramatic final moments put BC football on the modern map, and eventually even led to a breakfast cereal (Flutie Flakes), for goodness sake.

Flutie Magic

No one will ever know whether Doug Flutie, given the right set of circumstances, could have led a National Football League team to a championship. But there is no denying that the diminutive quarterback compiled a long and impressive record after he left Boston College.

When he got a legitimate shot in the NFL after an amazing run in the Canadian Football League, all Flutie did was lead the Buffalo Bills to the playoffs, earn a spot in the 1999 Pro Bowl, and take home the league's Comeback Player of the Year award.

Way back at the beginning of his pro career, he'd signed for big money with the USFL's New Jersey Generals and showed promise, only to see the league fold a year after he arrived. Flutie then played in a playoff game for the Chicago Bears before moving north of the border, where he eventually won three Grey Cups, led the league in passing five times, and earned six MVP awards.

Along the way, Flutie helped many charitable organizations and eventually established the Doug Flutie Jr. Autism Fund. That organization remains his passion in retirement, and it's just one of the things that makes him a beloved Boston sports star.

The game was filled with Flutie Magic, which longtime fans know began as far back as his days at Natick High School in Massachusetts. As an inexperienced sophomore quarterback, Flutie faced down a Braintree team that had roared back to lead by one point late in the game, and with only 21 seconds remaining, he fired four completions and kicked a 38-yard field goal for the win.

Ever since, Flutie Magic has been synonymous with perseverance in the most trying of times and with late-game heroics that defy all odds. The perpetually underestimated 11th-round draft pick has played professionally in the USFL, the NFL, and the CFL, and he has performed numerous miracles in every one of those leagues.

Still, he is a prisoner of The Pass. He is defined by a single moment, a schoolyard play that worked perfectly on a day when it seemed the whole world was watching. ❖

Andy Nesbitt, Globe Correspondent, contributed to this report.

Left: One of the best scramblers ever to play the game, Doug Flutie was Michael Vick before there was a Michael Vick.

> **"I just let it fly toward the pile — not necessarily toward Gerard Phelan, but where I thought everybody was going to be. I saw the ball go down over two defenders' heads and I thought it fell incomplete into the end zone."**
> **—DOUG FLUTIE**

Above (left to right): From pass to catch to celebration, TV has replayed (and replayed and replayed) this famous Hail Mary sequence. Screen images courtesy of CBS4 News, Boston.

THE CATCH

BY JANICE PAGE, GLOBE STAFF

He was one of those rare athletes who dared you to take your eyes off them for even a second. He was Michael Vick before Michael Vick; blink, and who knows what you'd miss.

How many other football players, or athletes for that matter, manage to hold on to the role of white knight for more than two decades, even after they start falling short more often than not? Until his very last play for the Patriots in 2005, when he converted the NFL's first successful drop-kick in 60-plus years, Doug Flutie had us all wondering what he might pull off next.

That's why when we thought of the Miracle in Miami, we usually thought of the BC quarterback. It's why all Flutie stories eventually came back to The Pass. But it's worth remembering that The Pass was also The Catch, and Gerald Phelan was the man who brought down the ball.

"The hard thing about the play was that the ball disappeared as everyone jumped up. . . I had to be a backstop, sort of like you catch a pencil rolling off the corner of the table," Phelan remembers. "The ball hit me just below the face mask and then into my chest, and I fell backwards. It was wet and it slid between my legs, so I curled my body up to stop it from getting all the way through... My first thought was: 'They're never going to let us get away with this in Miami on national television.'"

Phelan, a financial printing executive whose NFL career was cut short due to injury, sees no reason to be annoyed with folks who call it The Pass or focus on Flutie when they ask him (daily) to recollect the moment. "That's the pageantry of football," he says philosophically. "The hype, the grandeur, and all that other stuff."

In other words, quarterbacks get the glory.

In Phelan's eye, the Miracle in Miami is an oncoming ball falling from a sky of white rain. He may be the only one who remembers it this way, but that's what makes it his moment as well as Flutie's, and ours. ❖

FEBRUARY 22, 2000 » BY JOHN POWERS, GLOBE STAFF

OUR MIRACLE MEN ON ICE

he clock just wouldn't move. "There were 10 minutes left when I scored the goal," captain Mike Eruzione remembers. "I went out and played another shift and the clock said, like, 9:59. Then I played another shift and it said 8:20."

Time didn't stand still when the US Olympic hockey team shocked the Soviet Union and the world with its "Miracle on Ice" in Lake Placid, New York. It just seemed that way, as the Americans strove desperately to hold off the Big Red Machine until the last buzzer of the semifinal Olympic matchup.

In a sense, the game never did end. Millions of Americans held onto memories of where they were and what they were doing Feb. 22, 1980, when the Boys of Winter beat the unbeatable Soviets, 4-3, holding them scoreless for the final 37 minutes.

"It was a psychological turning point for the American people," says Jack O'Callahan, the defenseman from Charlestown, Massachusetts, whose exultant, toothless grin graces the famous celebratory photo snapped by The Boston Globe's Frank O'Brien. "Things were at a low point and the country was in a dark state."

In February of 1980, both inflation and unemployment were soaring, US citizens were being held hostage in Iran, the Red Army was defiantly occupying Afghanistan, and President Jimmy Carter was pushing for a boycott of the Summer Olympics in Moscow.

The Americans, seeded seventh among the 12-team field, weren't even supposed to win a medal on their home ice. They trailed in six of their seven games. They trailed the Soviets three times. They trailed the Finns with one period left to play in the final. But they never trailed at the end, which is all that matters.

At an average age of 22, this was the youngest US Olympic team ever. The Americans came from Massachusetts and the Midwest, from the shadow of Bunker Hill to the Iron Range of Minnesota. They were amateurs fresh out of college, most of them, or still undergrads. They were selected and molded and goaded and inspired by the mercurial, mystical Herb Brooks, the last player cut from the 1960 team that defeated the Soviets at Squaw Valley, California.

"We had the kind of team where if we didn't play well, we could lose to everybody in the tournament," says Jim Craig, the goalie from North Easton, Massachusetts, who played every minute of every game. "And if we did play well, we could beat everybody in the tournament."

Left: In this famous Globe photo, Bay State native Jack O'Callahan fell to his knees and roared, along with teammate Mike Ramsey, just after the underdog US team shocked the Soviets in the semifinal game.

WHO	**US** VS. **RUSSIA.**
WHERE	**LAKE PLACID, NEW YORK.**
WHEN	**FEBRUARY 22, 1980.**
WHY THE DRAMA	Hockey hadn't dominated the average American sports fan's consciousness before and it hasn't since. But for a short while, it was everything.

Bay State gold

It may have been a great victory for the US in general, but it was especially sweet for the small portion of it known as Massachusetts.

Boston area natives Mike Eruzione (Winthrop), the captain who scored the game-winner against the Soviets; Jim Craig (North Easton), the sturdy goalie who played every minute of every Olympic game; rugged defenseman Jack O'Callahan (Charlestown), and slick forward Dave Silk (Scituate) were all critical components of the team that captured America's heart. They were also the BU Quartet, because they all competed for Boston University.

O'Callahan went on to play in the National Hockey League with the Chicago Blackhawks, and he also established Beanpot Financial Futures with Jack Hughes (the last man cut from the 1980 Olympic hockey team) in the Windy City.

Eruzione, who essentially retired as a player after the gold-medal match with Finland, became a television commentator and motivational speaker. He was later named the director of athletic development at BU, where he also helped coach the hockey team.

After an up-and-down pro career, Craig went back to North Easton and became an account executive. And Silk, who played professionally in the NHL and Germany, became a Boston businessman.

Everybody, it seemed, except the guys in the red helmets. The Soviets were undeniably the best team in the world. A year earlier, the Soviets had beaten the cream of the NHL in a midseason best-of-three at Madison Square Garden, destroying the pros, 6-0, in the finale

The US Olympians also played the Soviets in the Garden in a tuneup the weekend before the Games and were demolished, 10-3. The Americans didn't figure to face the CCCP again. They weren't expected to make the Olympic medal round but then they tied the Swedes and beat Czechoslovakia 7-3.

"We began thinking, hey, we could take a medal out of this thing," says Dave Silk, who grew up in Scituate, Massachusetts. But the Soviets still loomed huge over everyone else. After all, they had won the gold at every Olympics since they first turned up in 1956. They hadn't lost a game since 1968.

But who knew what might happen in one night, one game, one chance. This was no accident, Brooks told his players before they took the ice for the semifinal game. This was fate.

"You were born to be a player," he said. "You were meant to be here. This moment is yours."

This was no mere hockey game, the Americans realized, as soon as they came out of their dressing room. It was, as Newsweek magazine said, "a morality play on ice."

"The flags were everywhere and they weren't bought on the way in," says Craig. "They brought them out of attics and basements. The patriotism at Lake Placid was real."

The Soviets scored first, after nine minutes, but that was no novelty. Everybody but the Romanians had scored first on the Americans. Buzz Schneider's slap shot tied it.

The Soviets grabbed the lead back within four minutes and set up shop in the US end, peppering Craig with rubber. Then, one second from the end of the first period, came the turning point. Dave Christian had taken a long,

what-the-hell slapper that bounced harmlessly off Vladislav Tretiak's pads. But Mark Johnson darted between a pair of Soviet defensemen and wristed in the rebound just before the buzzer.

The Soviets moved ahead again but then Johnson tied it again on a wrister from the slot. The Americans were staying stride for stride with the Soviets, banging and bollixing when the "Conehead Line" — Schneider, Mark Pavelich, and John Harrington from the Iron Range — was coming up ice and Schneider, out of gas, was lifting his stick to come off early.

Over the dasher came Eruzione, just in time to collect a pass from Pavelich. Eruzione saw defenseman Vasily Pervukhin go to one knee to block his shot and used the screen to light the lamp with a 25-footer.

The man who was almost cut a few months before the Games, the man who wasn't supposed to be on the ice, had put his mates within reach of the most astounding upset in hockey history, with 10 long minutes remaining.

Finally the final seconds ticked down, "Do you believe in miracles?" ABC announcer Al Michaels asked the nation, which was watching on tape delay because the international federation refused to change the 5:30 p.m. start. "Yes!," he shouted, as the buzzer sounded.

First, five teammates mobbed Craig, who had made 36 saves. Then, everyone on the bench came dashing onto the ice, hugging anyone in a white jersey. It didn't matter that there was still one game left to play — a gold-medal matchup that would end in a 4-2 victory over Finland.

Years, even decades later, Eruzione was still consistently running into people who insisted on telling him where they were when the US beat the Russians. "It's like Pearl Harbor and the Kennedy assassination and the Challenger. But those were terrible tragedies. Ours was a hockey game." And the good guys somehow won. ❖

Right: Captain Mike Eruzione, who was almost cut from the roster before the Olympics even started, ended up taking his team all the way.

ONE GIANT LEAP
FOR BRUINS FANS

On Mother's Day in 1970, a 22-year-old hockey prodigy flew through the rare air at the old Boston Garden after sliding the puck between the pads of Glenn Hall to deliver Boston's first Stanley Cup in 29 years.

Orr's brief flight capped off what most agree still stands as the most memorable professional hockey moment ever. Especially in Boston, of course, where at the time the Bruins were hockey's Beatles and the apostolic Orr had Paul's talent and John's soul.

Years later, Orr was often teased about the play's prominence. As video of the goal got more air play than Neil Armstrong's walk on the moon, there was some concern casual fans might not know that Orr accomplished a few other things on ice. At one point, when Orr appeared on TV with Ted Williams and Larry Bird, Williams asked him, "Is that the only goal you ever scored?"

"It (was) a good line," laughed Orr. "Glenn Hall (said) that to me every time he (saw) me."

The Bruins led the St. Louis Blues, three games to none when they played Game 4 at the Garden on a warm Sunday afternoon. It was 3-3 at the end of regulation, and 40 seconds into the first sudden-death overtime, Orr slid a pass to Derek Sanderson behind the net. Sanderson feathered the puck back to Orr as he crossed in front of Hall and Orr one-timed it between Hall's pads to clinch the Cup.

"Derek had a huge hand in the goal," says Orr. "In fact, he [professed] to have made my career.

"All I was trying to do was get it on goal. As I skated across, Glenn had to move across the crease and had to open his pads a little. When I shot it, I saw it got in, so I jumped. Then Noel Picard helped a little by lifting his stick under my skate."

Picard's chippy move served only to add to the drama. ❖

Left: Bruins goalie Gerry Cheevers (left) embraced the hero, Bobby Orr, after the game.
Right: It was an era of Garden champagne parties and a moment when the Bruins ruled Boston. Yes, it was a long time ago.

WHO	**BRUINS** VS. **BLUES.**
WHERE	**BOSTON GARDEN.**
WHEN	**MAY 10, 1970.**
WHY THE DRAMA	Extensive research has shown that the Game 4 overtime tally wasn't the only goal scored in the 1970 Stanley Cup Finals. It only seems that way.

A team effort, really

The man who actually led the Bruins in playoff scoring was Phil Esposito, who set NHL records with 13 goals and 14 assists as Boston first defeated the New York Rangers in six games and then blasted through a pair of four-game sweeps. The whole season was a Garden party, featuring 38 straight sellouts and a 17-game home unbeaten streak. After tying the Chicago Blackhawks for most regular-season points (99), the Bruins beat them 4-0 in the playoffs' second round.

THE LEGEND OF BOBBY ORR

DECEMBER 29, 1999 ❱❱ KEVIN PAUL DUPONT, GLOBE STAFF

> "Is that the only goal you ever scored?"
>
> —TED WILLIAMS, to Bobby Orr

There was a style to Bobby Orr's game, a raw yet graceful ferocity, that was his essence. Decades after he last pulled on his No. 4 Bruins sweater for a full season of work, Orr's career is easily quantified by all the awards he won, the points he scored, the Stanley Cups he raised, even the money he made.

But the numbers are such a small part of his story. Orr was so much more than what he did. "Nureyev on ice," the late Globe columnist Ray Fitzgerald once wrote. And his best move?

"Putting on his [expletive] skates," grunted Gordie Howe, the greatest the game had seen, nicknamed Mr. Hockey, until Orr came along.

Orr arrived in Boston from Parry Sound, Ontario, in the fall of '66 with the brush-cut hair and wide-eyed innocence of a dog-faced G.I. Pursued by the Bruins from adolescence, he was the NHL's most valuable player for the first time in 1970, all of 10 years after the likes of Milt Schmidt, Lynn Patrick, and Weston Adams first spotted him as a 12-year-old in a bantam championship game. It was in part a promise by the Bruins to paint his family home that convinced Orr to sign with Boston.

Before his arrival, NHL defensemen rarely joined the play, tethered by job description to the front of their net in their own end and to the blue line in the attacking zone. Orr opened up the game with his blazing speed and deft, almost eerie anticipation, streaking all over the ice, posing an offensive threat from the moment his stick — with but a one-inch strip of black tape wrapped mid-blade — touched the puck behind his own net.

He would rocket past defenders on power plays, toy with forechecking forwards in a game of keep-away when killing penalties, pull fans out of their seats, and cause opposing coaches to yank tufts of hair from their heads. The days of plodding, stay-home defensemen were changed forever, and the ice surface was stretched wide, as if held up to a funhouse looking glass.

"It wasn't fair that he was made to play with us," said the Flyers' pugnacious and talented Bobby Clarke, an arch-enemy in the heated days of the great Boston-Philadelphia rivalry. "There should have been a higher league for him to go to."

And he did score that one magnificent goal in particular. In the instant after the 1970 Stanley Cup clincher, Orr was in full celebration before most of the sellout Garden crowd on that hot, steamy Mother's Day was aware the game had ended. It was quintessential Orr — seizing the moment ahead of everyone else.

In the thick of his career, even while knee injuries began to blunt the edge from his game, Orr obliterated the NHL record book. The MVP in 1970 was his first of three consecutive Hart Trophies. In '68, at the end of only his second NHL season, he won his first of eight consecutive Norris Trophies as the game's best defenseman, a record likely never to be surpassed.

Consider: No defenseman ever had scored more than 20 goals prior to his arrival; Orr more than doubled that (46). He was the first defenseman ever to score 100 points, which he did for six consecutive seasons, far surpassing the league's previous one-season high of 59 points by a blue liner. ❖

Above: Thousands of fans turned out to show their appreciation for Orr and company.

Above: Number 4's great leap of a goal was the biggest hockey moment in Boston. It still is.

HAVLICEK STOLE THE BALL

"*All right, Greer's putting the ball into play . . . He gets it out deep and Havlicek steals it! Over to Sam Jones! Havlicek stole the ball! It's all over! Johnny Havlicek is being mobbed by the fans. It's all over! Johnny Havlicek stole the ball! Oh, boy, what a play by Havlicek at the end of this ballgame! Johnny Havlicek stole the ball on the pass-in. Oh, my, what a play by Havlicek! A spectacular series comes to an end in spectacular fashion! John Havlicek being hoisted aloft . . . He yells and waves his hands. Bill Russell wants to grab Havlicek . . . He hugs him.*
He squeezes John Havlicek. Havlicek saved this ballgame. Believe that! Johnny Havlicek saved this ballgame. The Celtics win it, 110-109. We'll be back with our wrap-up in just one minute!"

That was Johnny Most's call of the final moments of the seventh game of the Eastern Conference finals played at the Boston Garden in April of 1965.

It's the single most famous chapter of Boston Celtics history and it was over in an instant. John Havlicek knocked away an inbounds pass and immediately went from Nice Player to Legend, abetted by the most famous basketball radio call ever. Forget Boston. This is the most famous call in NBA history. I mean, let's get real. There was only one Johnny Most.

"It was a memorable night," deadpanned Red Auerbach several decades later.

Ya' think?

It was, as Most so accurately described, "a spectacular series" coming to an end "in spectacular fashion." The Bill Russell-led Celtics and the Wilt Chamberlain-led 76ers had battled evenly in the Eastern Conference finals for six games, 47 minutes, and 56 seconds. The Celtics were clinging to a 1-point lead with four seconds left, but the 76ers were putting the ball in play under their basket after Russell made the boo-boo of all boo-boos, hitting a guide wire on an inbounds pass after a Chamberlain stuff had made the score 110-109, and thus turning the ball back over to the Sixers.

Above: Johnny Most got his props at the Garden.
Right: John Havlicek spent the better part of two decades in a Celtics uniform, and he never once let up until the final whistle.

Basketball

WHO	**CELTICS** VS. **76ERS.**
WHERE	**BOSTON GARDEN.**
WHEN	**APRIL 15, 1965.**
WHY THE DRAMA	A stickler for detail would have said, "Havlicek tips it! Over to Sam Jones for the steal! Havlicek tipped the ball!" But who likes sticklers?

Hondo's legacy

It took one play for John Havlicek to become a legend, but 16 years of memorable moments are what makes him one of the best players in NBA history.

Over the course of his career, this Celtic superstar amassed statistics that still sit at or near the top of Celtic and NBA record books. But it was his immeasurable contribution to the franchise over the long haul that led Red Auerbach to declare him "the measure of what it means to be a Celtic."

Neatly bridging the gap between the Bill Russell and Dave Cowens eras, the inexhaustible Havlicek was an integral member of eight championship teams, a 6-foot-5-inch, 205-pound guard/forward who came to be known as the ultimate sixth man.

Havlicek's career averages — 20.8 points, 6.3 rebounds, 4.8 assists — are not dazzling. But his work ethic and efficiency in the clutch allowed him to develop into a 13-time All-Star and a five-time member of the All-NBA defensive first team.

Even decades after his retirement, Havlicek's consistency and longevity enabled him to still lead all Celtics in games played, minutes played, points, field goals made and attempted, and free throws made and attempted. His number, 17, was raised to the Garden rafters in 1978.

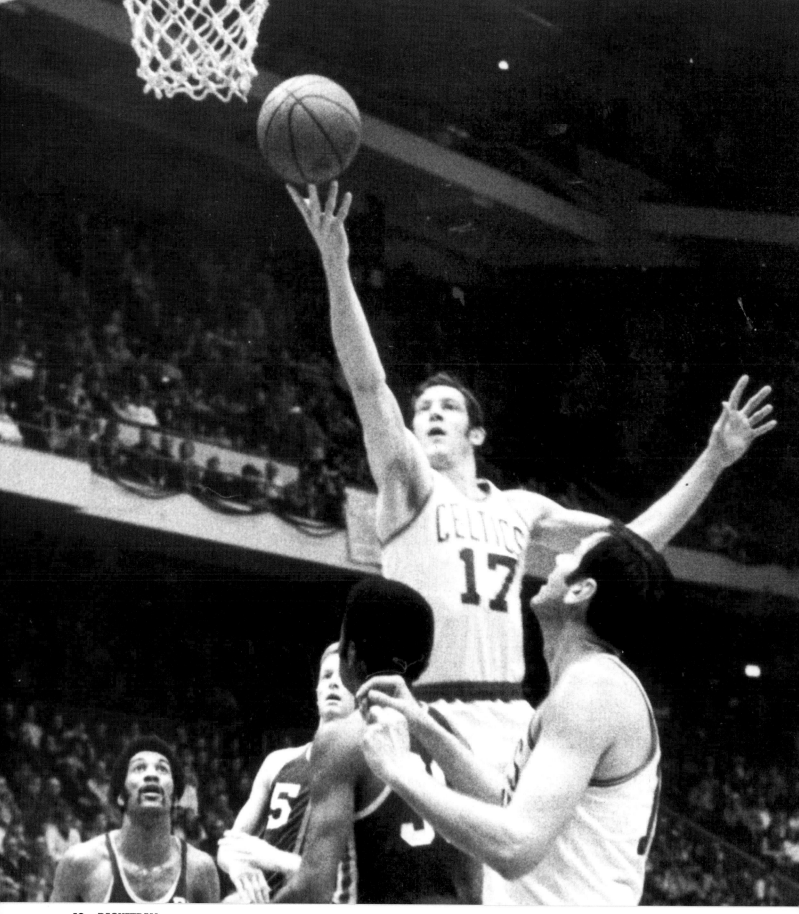

I can hear the young'uns out there: "What's a guide wire?"

Hey, it was 1965, and this was the beloved Boston Garden. The backboard was supported by wires that ran from the edge of the backboard up to the first balcony. It was one of those wires that Russell hit.

"Russell was in the huddle saying, 'I screwed up,' " recalls Tom Heinsohn, then a guy with a bad foot playing in his penultimate series. "'Somebody get me off the hook.'"

Somebody did. Hal Greer took the ball out of bounds. Sam Jones was on him. Russell was, of course, guarding Wilt, who already had 30 points and 32 rebounds. Satch Sanders was guarding burly Luke Jackson. K.C. Jones was guarding the 6-foot-10-inch Johnny Kerr. And John Havlicek was guarding Chet Walker.

The Celtics had a lot of things to worry about and four long seconds to worry about them. Walker was a great shooter. Jackson had that colossal size mismatch with the 6-1 Jones. Greer, one of the great middle jump shooters ever, could take a return pass from anyone and become an instant threat. Chamberlain could take a pass and dunk one. And Chamberlain, Kerr, and Jackson could crash the boards if a shot was missed.

None of it materialized. Greer tried to throw it in to Walker, and Havlicek, reading the play perfectly, tipped the ball in the direction of Sam Jones, who dribbled into a mob that had swarmed onto the court. "I went up, but I couldn't get control of it," Havlicek said in a 1985 interview. "I saw Sam going the other way and, fortunately, nobody was in a position to foul him."

"What's interesting," said longtime Celtic TV voice Mike Gorman, who was in the stands as a fan that night, "is that if you saw the play, you would never say that Havlicek 'stole' the ball. He 'deflected' the ball. But Johnny Most said he 'stole' the ball, and that was that."

The game and the series were over. But The Legend was just about to take shape, thanks to Most and thanks to Jess Cain, who played the call over and over the next morning on his immensely popular WHDH (850) morning show, and thanks to a subsequent highlight album put out by Fleetwood Records.

The Celtics were en route to a seventh consecutive championship (they would wipe out the Lakers in five for the title), but they were more of a cult than a local sports fixture until this play and Most's call.

It was an entirely different Boston. There was hardly a skyline. Cardinal Cushing was The Man. The Red Sox were pathetic, drawing fewer than 700,000 to a ballpark everyone agreed was a dump. Three hundred people ran the Marathon; the winner got a handshake and a laurel wreath, and everyone who finished got a bowl of beef stew.

And the NBA had nine teams.

No one could possibly have envisioned the NBA of today, with its flash and glitter, with its lights-out intros and booming music. Back then, John Kiley would rouse the crowd by playing the "Mexican Hat Dance" on the organ.

It was all innocent, but it was eminently accessible. It was about the basketball, not about The Show. And the basketball was pretty darn good.

"All the players back then were masters of the fundamentals, which allowed them to be creative," Heinsohn explains. "They were jazz groups. And now we have orchestras with music right in front of them. Some of these guys even ask the coach to turn the pages of the music for them."

Still, one of today's players might get lucky enough to enjoy a moment like John Havlicek's. The only problem is he won't have a broadcasting maestro like Johnny Most to make him an instant legend. ❖

> "All the players back then were masters of the fundamentals, which allowed them to be creative. They were jazz groups. And now we have orchestras with music right in front of them."
>
> —TOM HEINSOHN

Left: Havlicek didn't just steal (OK, deflect) balls for a living; he mastered every fundamental of the sport. And he was a thing of beauty when he went in for a layup under a crowded basket.

A MARATHON RIVALRY THAT WENT TO THE WIRE

She was wheeling toward the finish line, alone it seemed, and she heard the public address announcer tell the assembled masses that she was about to win her eighth Boston Marathon in the woman's wheelchair division.

It was going to be a sweet victory in the wake of the previous year's (1997) trolley track spill.

But just before Jean Driscoll crossed the line, her rival Louise Sauvage whizzed by Driscoll's right wheel and broke the tape. Both women were timed in 1:41:19, but Sauvage was the winner, by less then the length of a wheelchair.

"I was just getting ready to throw my arms up and she came by," Driscoll said after this defeat of Red Soxian proportion. "I'm still shocked."

Shocked, but not bitter. Beaten, but not deflated. Driscoll did not cry and could not have been more gracious.

Maybe it's because she grew up with spina bifida and could never run like the other kids. Maybe it's because she used up her ravaged leg muscles by the time she was 15 and learned to live in a wheelchair. Maybe it's because she had competed in these races since she was 20 years old and had learned to accept defeat as part of competition.

Or maybe it was just the way she was — a charming, unassuming, gritty young woman who grew up in Wisconsin.

We had found out a little something about Driscoll the year before. She'd won seven consecutive women's wheelchair titles in Boston and had a chance to unseat the legendary Clarence DeMar as the winningest competitor in the history of the race.

On that fateful day, she was hubcap-to-hubcap with Australia's Sauvage when she roared into Cleveland Circle. She looked like she could ride forever on the streets of Boston. Then she met the foe that has flattened hundreds of cyclists and pedestrians through the years — the MBTA trolley tracks.

Driscoll flipped her chair. A total 180. She got some assistance from race officials, but it took more than five minutes to get her back on course, and even then she had to race the rest of the way with a flat tire and a scraped elbow. But she never complained and she still finished second to Sauvage.

In the rematch, Driscoll kept pace in the early miles, then turned on the burners after making the right turn at the firehouse that marks the base of the Newton Hills. By the time she finished with the hills, she couldn't see anybody behind her.

Left: In 1998, Jean Driscoll never saw Louise Sauvage coming until it was too late, and the Australian looked as though she couldn't quite believe it herself as she hit the tape. Right: The two fierce competitors share an emotional hug after the race.

BOSTON MARATHON / WOMEN'S WHEELCHAIR DIVISION

WHO	**JEAN DRISCOLL** VS. **LOUISE SAUVAGE.**
WHERE	**HOPKINTON TO BOSTON.**
WHEN	**APRIL 20, 1998.**
WHY THE DRAMA	It was a competitor's worst nightmare. Victory seemingly assured — the race announcer even said so — just inches from the finish line…. then, whoosh!

Elite eight

Jean Driscoll has won just about every award imaginable, including two Olympic medals, 12 Paralympic medals, and the Women's Sports Foundation's Sportswoman of the Year. She was ranked No. 25 on Sports Illustrated for Women's list of The Top 100 Female Athletes of the 20th Century. Heck, in 2003, she was even named Godmother of Royal Caribbean International's Voyager Class ship, Mariner of the Seas.

This incredible competitor, who earned undergraduate and graduate degrees from the University of Illinois, has also focused considerable energy on working with disabled athletes in Ghana, West Africa. Her Determined to Win fund collects donations to buy new racing equipment for the athletes.

But her forearms tightened in the final couple of miles and Sauvage, a renowned sprinter, started to gain. Still, when Driscoll made the final left run onto Boylston Street, she checked behind her and felt safe. She had Sauvage by about 50 meters.

If Driscoll had had a rear-view mirror, she might have won. If she only had known how fast Sauvage was coming, maybe she could have found an extra ounce for one last push.

Instead, Driscoll didn't know what to do after she crossed the line, so she sat in her chair and leaned forward, trying to process what had just happened. Then Sauvage wheeled to her side and the rivals embraced.

Shortly thereafter Sauvage shivered with excitement as she relived those last seconds of her spectacular victory.

"I think back when I was getting closer and closer to Jean," she said. "I thought, 'maybe,' and then, 'I could make it,' and then, 'I did make it.' It was unreal.

"Then again, I thought of what I preach to kids: Never quit, never quit, never quit. I'm glad I listened to the advice I give others."

"It's a huge deal to lose this," said Driscoll. "But we have a strong mutual respect for each other. Any time you get on the starting line, you put your reputation on the line. It's racing.

"There was a lot of stress and anticipation before this race. Boston means a lot. I love the town and the race, and the fans are wonderful."

They cheered for her all the way. They roared when she crossed the tracks at Cleveland Circle without a spill. And they applauded her when she finished second to an equally worthy opponent. ❖

Bob Monahan, Globe Staff, contributed to this report

Above: In another incredibly close race, Sauvage finished just ahead of Driscoll in 1999.
Right: Finally in 2000, Driscoll took home her record eighth first-place trophy. And this time, she was all smiles.

More heartbreak and joy

April 18, 2000

BY TONY CHAMBERLAIN, GLOBE STAFF

Jean Driscoll waited a few yards beyond the finish of the 2000 Boston Marathon before raising her arms with a series of hearty whoops and a few "Praise God!" shouts. Two years prior, as she began a premature celebration, archrival Louise Sauvage shot past her to take the tape in a photo finish.

But this time around, Driscoll finally got over the hurdle that had stopped her from winning a record eighth divisional victory — namely, the 26-year-old Australian, Sauvage.

Driscoll, who also defeated a cold easterly headwind, finished in 2 hours 52 seconds, with Sauvage just 24 seconds behind and closing fast.

With the victory, Driscoll broke her tie with Clarence DeMar for most wins in one Boston division. DeMar, the legendary Melrose runner, won the men's race seven times between 1911 and 1930.

"I was scared stiff the whole last mile," said Driscoll, whose nemesis, Sauvage, won three straight Boston championships of her own. "I kept expecting her to catch up."

The cold wind made the race particularly tough, especially when the lighter Driscoll was buffeted on the downhills.

"It was bad the whole race," she said. "I was getting frustrated on the downhills. I'd look back and she'd be catching up.

"I'm so extremely happy," said Driscoll, shivering beneath a blanket at the finish. "I've waited for this a long time. But winning with competition like Louise makes this win legitimate."

From 1990 to '96, Driscoll won Boston seven straight times. At the time, she heard criticism that the division was not competitive. But then Sauvage, seven years younger, appeared on the scene and ended Driscoll's streak, winning the next three years straight.

In 1999, Driscoll spotted Sauvage about 50 yards early on but came on strong at the end, only to lose in a photo finish. That race marked the second straight year the race was so close the two competitors were credited with the same time.

EASY RYDER? NOT THIS TIME

They'd been left for dead the night before the final round, derided by many of their own fans as choking millionaires with no team spirit. But the United States golfers climbed defiantly out of their gilded coffins at The Country Club in Brookline, Massachusetts, and ripped the Ryder Cup away from the Europeans, 14 1/2 points to 13 1/2 points, in one of the greatest comebacks in sporting history.

"Darned if we didn't pull it off," exulted champagne-drenched US captain Ben Crenshaw. He did so after Justin Leonard came from four holes down with seven to play to sink a monster putt on the fabled 17th green on the way to halving his match with two-time Masters champion Jose Maria Olazabal. In so doing he returned the golden chalice to the Americans for the first time since 1993.

"It's unbelievable," Crenshaw marveled.

It was a bitter defeat for the Europeans, who led in points, 10-6, after two days of foursome and four-ball matches and needed to win only 4 of the 12 singles matches in the final day to retain the Cup that was first put into competition by Samuel Ryder at Worcester CC in 1927. They could only come up with 3 1/2.

Each match of the 28 played over three days counted for one point, with half-points given when matches ended in a tie. No team had ever come from so far back to win the Cup.

But once the the Americans had claimed yesterday's first six matches — most notably David Duval's 5-holes-up-with-4-holes-remaining flogging of unbeaten Jesper Parnevik — they suddenly found themselves with 11 points to the Europeans' 10. From there they rode a wave of emotion and euphoria to victory.

"It happened like a dream," Crenshaw said. "It was just like a force was pulling us together."

Left: David Duval took his time lining up a shot on the 16th green.
Right: Team USA 's Justin Leonard was understandably exuberant after sinking a long putt on hole 15 during his match with Jose Maria Olazabal.

Golf

THE RYDER CUP

WHO	**US** VS. **EUROPE.**
WHERE	**THE COUNTRY CLUB,** BROOKLINE, MASSACHUSETTS.
WHEN	**SEPTEMBER 26, 1999.**
WHY THE DRAMA	Europe seemed unbeatable. The US seemed indifferent. Everything changed in the final round.

As good as it gets

Who knew golf could be like this?

Golf: the "Good Walk Spoiled." Golf: the sport of the privileged and the elite. Golf: the sport for fat people, skinny people, uncoordinated people, and just plain unathletic people.

Even the people who say such things have to admit that what took place at the 1999 Ryder Cup was one of the most unbelievable (for once the truly appropriate term) events ever to take place in Brookline, Greater Boston, Massachusetts, and even the US of A. The US team didn't just defeat the Europeans, they moidered da bums. They knew what was at stake and they reacted with all the emotional savagery of a Rockne-inspired football squad. This wasn't golf. This was tourist abuse.

"The putts were just going in from all angles," said European captain Mark James with a sigh. "And the chips. Perhaps I could have rung up a bomb scare. Maybe that would have stopped it."

"We dominated," said Davis Love III. " We got the momentum going and we started playing as a team."

Momentum? It was a tsunami. The great American shots and the ever-increasing run of red numbers on the scoreboard got the crowd of some 30,000 into it. There were no more comments about being stiffed for autographs by the haughty Americans. In the end, it was all red, white, and blue kisses. And golf, the way it should be played.

Above: Champagne rained down from a balcony of The Country Club.

This was a US team almost torn apart by the issue of money, but it was talent, emotion, and genuine feeling that led to this triumph of triumphs. Duval, who had been criticized for his comments regarding Ryder Cup compensation, responded with his clubs. "I was sick and tired of everybody saying we weren't a team," said Duval.

Said Phil Mickelson, a 4-and-3 winner over Jarmo Sandelin, "We not only won, we dominated. We won big in the first four matches."

This was truly American golf in its highest form. Tom Lehman beat Lee Westwood of Great Britain, 3 and 2; Hal Sutton beat Darren Clarke of Northern Ireland, 4 and 2; Mickelson rolled; Davis Love whipped Jean Van de Velde of France, 6 and 5; and Tiger Woods won three holes in a row to close out the front side en route to a 3-and-2 win over Andrew Coltart of Scotland. Duval made it six straight.

There were some eyebrows raised when European captain Mark James sat down Sandelin, Van de Velde, and Coltart in the first four matches, then sent them out to play matches No. 3, No. 4, and No. 5 yesterday. By the time Dubliner Padraig Harrington kept the European hopes alive by beating Mark O'Meara 1 up, time was running out. Steve Pate beat Spain's Miguel Angel Jimenez, 2 and 1, and Jim Furyk handed Spanish teenage sensation Sergio Garcia his first defeat in five matches (3-1-1), 4 and 3. Leonard then did his thing before losing the 18th hole to halve the match, but his half-point put the Americans over the top.

This competition was rejuvenated in 1979 when all of Europe became a part of it. Players such as Nick Faldo, Seve Ballesteros, Bernhard Langer, Ian Woosnam, and Olazabal joined the fray and quickly came of age. But nothing prepared anyone for what transpired in 1999. It was magical. ❖

Joe Concannon, Globe Staff, contributed to this report.

Right: Tiger Woods was as pumped as his audience after he chipped in a shot at the 8th hole during his match with Andrew Coltart.

WORLD CUP WONDERFUL

They'd surely never heard of Yogi's Law, and if you started talking about the night that Larry stole Zeke's inbounds pass to save a playoff game you'd get nothing but blank stares in downtown Lagos.

But if you know anything about "it ain't over till it's over" lessons learned in New England, you have to empathize with the Nigerian soccer team, which shoulda/coulda/woulda beat Italy in elimination-round World Cup soccer action in Foxborough, if only . . .

How close was Nigeria to victory? We'll never know exactly, because this is FIFA football and they're still living with this quaint 19th century notion of injury time, an absurdity so idiotic as to defy any sort of rational analysis in this digital era. Anyway, the score was Nigeria 1, Italy 0 and we were in the 89th minute in a 90-minute game (plus however many minutes the referee might have added on) when disaster struck the team known as the Super Eagles.

"It was a very good match," sighed Nigerian coach Clemens Westerhof. "Victory was two minutes too far away." With victory that close, Nigeria should have been zealots, absolute maniacs, on defense. But resourceful Italy, playing with 10 men after Gianfranco Zola was red-carded in the 76th minute, was able to mount one more offensive surge, culminating in a pretty Roberto Mussi feed and a goal by Italian superhero Roberto Baggio. Forevermore, the Nigerians will know that it ain't over till Yogi says it is.

Dejected, stunned, shocked, crushed, and deflated, the Nigerians were never the same again. The record book will show that Italy prevailed thanks to a Baggio penalty kick in the 102d minute. Reality is that Italy won the game the minute the Azzurri gained the tie in that 89th minute.

"We were supposed to win, you know?" said Nigeria's Finidi George. "We had the opportunities."

For Italy, which was eliminated from 1990 World Cup play by Argentine penalty kicks, this victory represented a phone call from the governor at the 11th hour and 59th minute. The last meal had been eaten. The chaplain had paid his visit. The burly guard was at the cell and the Last Long Walk was about to begin. Italy was going down, and with good reason. The Nigerians had taken a 1-nil lead at intermission and had spent the entire second half pistol-whipping the embarrassed Italians upside the head.

The Nigerians enjoyed major second-half territorial domination. Italy just couldn't get the ball often enough to do anything on offense. Augustine (Jay Jay) Okocha was beating the proud Italians all by himself with his astounding footwork. With each passing minute the drums in the Nigerian section of the stands were getting more and more into it, and it was getting very easy to envision the North End, populated of course by more than a few fans of the team that found itself in increasingly dire straits, as one vast funeral parlor.

Except that it ain't over till it's over.

The World Cup always has main plots and subplots and in 1994 the basic subplot was the rise of new powers. The United States opened a few eyes with its quite respectable play, and so, too, did Nigeria assert itself in the world arena. The Super Eagles had never been to the World Cup before, but once they arrived, they did some damage.

Afterwards, the Nigerians expected to go home and receive acclaim for what they'd done. They got out of the first round and they came within a minute or two of taking out a team with one of the great football pedigrees. You know who they were? They were UMass; that's who. They were (1994 NCAA men's basketball tournament upstart) UMass, and Italy was (favored) Kentucky, and neither UMass nor Nigeria quite knew how to close the deal. ❖

Right: Italian superstar Roberto Baggio struggled with the Nigerian defense for most of the day.

Soccer

WHO	**ITALY** VS. **NIGERIA.**
WHERE	**FOXBORO STADIUM,** FOXBOROUGH, MASSACHUSETTS.
WHEN	**JULY 5, 1994.**
WHY THE DRAMA	Nigeria was on the verge of one of the biggest upsets in soccer history. Italy was a man down. The 87th minute ticked away, then the 88th and… uh oh.

Just for kicks

Globe sportswriter Frank Dell'Apa ranks the best games played in the Boston area.

1. April 19, 1927 Boston Wonder Workers 3, Uruguay 2 at Malden High School. Powerhouse Uruguay came up short; Barney Battles scored twice for Boston. The game turned into a brawl in the second half and was stopped with 10 minutes remaining.

2. July 5, 1994 Italy 2, Nigeria 1 (OT) at Foxboro Stadium.

3. June 20, 1975 - Minutemen 2, Cosmos 1 at Richardson (now Nickerson) Field. Billed as Eusebio (Minutemen) vs. recently signed Pele. A Pele goal was disallowed, the crowd invaded the field, and the NASL nullified the result.

4. May 30, 1931 New York Yankees 4, Celtic 3 at Fenway Park. Billy Gonsalves scored three goals for the Yankees in what legendary Celtic manager Willie Maley called "the greatest performance I have ever seen."

5. July 9, 1994 Italy 2, Spain 1 at Foxboro Stadium.

6. June 16, 1972 Benfica 2, Sporting 2 at Foxboro Stadium. Response to this game was so great that a rematch was scheduled a week later.

7. March 29, 1925 Boston Wonder Workers 2, Fall River Marksmen 1 at Mark's Stadium, Tiverton, R.I. Alec McNab, considered the Pele of era, scored the deciding goal of the Lewis Cup final in Boston's first American Soccer League season.

8. June 16, 1980 Tea Men 2, Cosmos 1 at Foxboro Stadium. Salif Keita of Mali bended in a free kick for the winner, one of the most skillful goals in stadium history.

9. Oct. 20, 1996 D.C. United 3, LA Galaxy 2 (OT) at Foxboro Stadium. The first MLS Cup final, nearly postponed because of a torrential downpour.

10. Aug. 7, 1994 US 4, Norway 1 at Fitton Field, Worcester. Michelle Akers at height of her powers; Mia Hamm scored twice.

Above left: **Nigerian goalkeeper Peter Rufai had his hands full once the Italian offense found its feet in the final minutes.**

Above right: **Outplayed until it was nearly too late, the Italian side had to be thrilled, not to mention relieved, that they managed to pull this one out.**

Another thriller

BY FRANK DELL'APA, GLOBE STAFF

Roberto Baggio retained his scoring touch and his sense of drama when Italy recorded another victory in the next round. The Azzurri defeated Spain 2-1.

Baggio scored the winning goal in the 88th minute before a crowd of 54,605 in the last Foxboro Stadium match of the 15th World Cup. Italy went on to defeat Bulgaria in a semifinal but then lost the final to Brazil on penalty kicks.

After his stellar performance saved the day against the Nigerians in the previous round, fans might have wondered what Baggio could possibly do for an encore. What he did was turn the game around with one electrifying run. Up until then, the Spanish team that was a victory away from its best World Cup finish since 1950 had thoroughly outplayed its European rivals.

To kick off the critical sequence, Baggio took a pass in full stride from Giuseppe Signori. He then rounded charging goalkeeper Andoni Zubizarreta and blasted the ball into the back of the net.

"I am not surprised when Baggio does positive things," Italian goalkeeper Gianluca Pagliuca said. "Only when he does negative things."

It was Pagliuca, making a remarkable reappearance after having been suspended for two games because of a foul against Norway, who held down the fort at the other end of the pitch.

The Italians had survived quite well with his replacement, Luca Marchegiani. But Marchegiani never was tested like Pagliuca was against Spain. He made three spectacular saves. The first was a diving grab of a 25-yard drive by Juan Antonio Goikoetxea in the 61st minute, a play that depended on Pagliuca's alertness and positioning. The second save was on Julio Salinas, who broke through the Italian defense into the penalty area in the 83d minute — Pagliuca challenged Salinas, raised his hands as if to dive to the right, and stopped Salinas' shot with his left foot. Two minutes later, Pagliuca tipped a 30-yard bullet by Fernando Hierro over the bar.

Italy's less-well-known Baggio, Dino, had given the Azzurri the initial lead. But Spain's Jose Jose Luis Caminero's tied it up with a left-footed drive in the 59th minute, setting up Roberto Baggio's repeat performance in the waning minutes.

HAGLER TKO'S HEARNS IN 3

Below: Marvelous Marvin's barrage of third-round punches knocked his opponent to the canvas and earned him a middleweight belt.

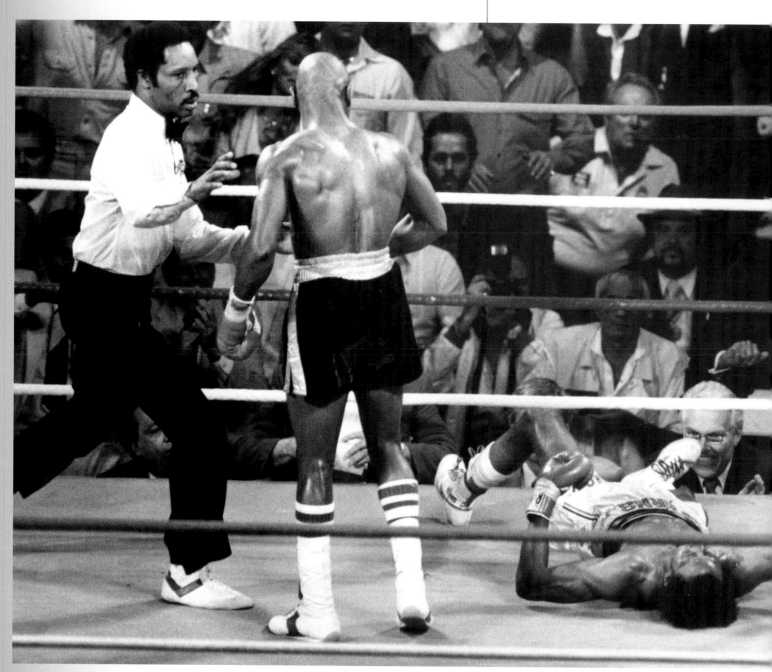

Each fighter went for the knockout from the opening bell, loading up every punch with as much strength as he could muster and hammering the other across the ring. Neither fighter had much of an edge in the first two rounds, but both seemed to somehow sense that this Las Vegas brawl would not, indeed could not, last long.

A world middleweight championship was on the line but what had really turned up the heat was weeks of pre-fight trash-talking between the camps of Marvelous Marvin Hagler and Thomas "Hitman" Hearns.

"Marvin always talked himself into disliking his opponent, and by the end of that two weeks, he hated Tommy," said promoter Bob Arum. "And Tommy wasn't the kind of guy to take a backward step, so he hated Marvin back."

When it was over, Hagler had retained his world middleweight championship by stopping Hearns on a technical knockout in the third round of the title defense. By any measure the bout was a defining moment in Hagler's storied career.

The champ stopped the challenger at 2:01 of the third after landing three right hands that sent him to the canvas and left him foggy when he struggled to his feet at the count of 10. When Hearns could not raise his hands to defend himself, referee Richard Steele stopped the fight.

WHO	**MARVIN HAGLER** VS. **THOMAS HEARNS.**
WHERE	**CAESARS PALACE,** LAS VEGAS.
WHEN	**APRIL 15, 1985.**
WHY THE DRAMA	After weeks of verbal sparring, the fighters nearly saw their bout called short when Hearns opened a cut above Hagler's eye. But Hagler wasn't done.

Moving on

Plenty of boxers have gone to great lengths to get the fight game out of their system. But few went as far as "The Marvelous One."

Several jaded years after his bitter final loss to Sugar Ray Leonard, Marvin Hagler decided to relocate… to Italy. And if that didn't surprise Boston boxing fans enough, we were definitely floored to find out that he went abroad to be — of all things — an actor.

He's made some Italian films playing a military officer, a cop, and a terrorist, but he claims he has no intention of ever playing a boxer. "I want to branch out and play a doctor or a lawyer," he said in a 2006 story by Globe correspondent Robert Carroll. "I love acting."

Hagler's reputation as a standup guy, proudly touted in his hometown of Brockton, Massachusetts, has apparently followed him to Milan, where he has a whole new flock of admirers. He has stayed involved in a host of charitable endeavors, including working with the International Brotherhood of Electrical Workers to fight homelessness, traveling to Argentina to help keep kids off drugs, and annually hosting the Marvelous Marvin Hagler Boxing Tournament for his own charitable foundation, which helps young adults find vocational education.

To us, Marvelous Marvin will always be a Brockton boy at heart. Even if he speaks with an Italian flourish and ends conversations with a warm "Arriverderci."

It was the 11th consecutive successful defense for Hagler, who managed to extend the run of Brockton, Massachusetts as the "City of Champions." Of course that run had begun a couple decades earlier when Brockton native Rocky Marciano grabbed hold of the heavyweight championship and never let it go — in the ring, at least.

In the Hagler-Hearns matchup, Hagler was initially rocked by a deep cut to his forehead that put his title in jeopardy from the first round on.

Near the middle of the second round, Hagler looked withered but still managed to force the challenger backward. He was carrying the fight to the ropes — the last place Hearns wanted to be. With Hearns on the retreat, Hagler gained the upper hand, slipping blows and pressuring inside to Hearns's body. At the bell, Hearns appeared to be in trouble.

Hearns came out for the third round on his toes, boxing Hagler with both hands and trying to keep him at a distance. A series of slashing blows reopened Hagler's forehead cut, and ringside physician Donald Romeo was called in to examine the champion. In a key decision, the fight was allowed to continue.

When action resumed Hagler knew there wasn't much time left, so he lumbered a leaping right hook on Hearns's chin that sent the challenger reeling.

Hagler chased him to the ropes and slammed in two more explosive right hooks as Hearns went down flat on his back. Gamely, Hearns pulled himself up, but it wasn't convincing enough. This time, Steele had no choice but to stop the bout. ❖

MARVELOUS MARVIN ENSHRINED

BY RON BORGES, GLOBE STAFF

*I*t seems fitting that the climax of Marvelous Marvin Hagler's boxing career happened in the same kind of small-town arena where so much of it was spent.

In 1993, when Hagler was inducted into the International Boxing Hall of Fame in Canastota, New York, he was honored in just the kind of place where he struggled for seven long years to make someone notice him: Brockton, Portland, New Bedford (on a night when he fought a guy named Peachy Davis), Taunton, Hartford, Providence. These were the backwater towns where a fighting machine would be built that would rule the middleweight division for 7 1/2 years. There and on the winter beaches around Provincetown, Massachusetts, where he would go to train with only Pat and Goody Petronelli, his sparring partners and the demons that drove him at his side.

Provincetown's snow-covered beaches were his desolate retreat — lonely, quiet places next to an angry sea. It was a perfect setting for the monastic life of a professional boxer that Hagler believed in for so long, before the big money and the Las Vegas glitz took over near the end of his career.

Eventually he would leave those towns and get his chance to fight Vito Antuofermo in 1979 for the title he had chased for half his career, but only after the intervention of Congressmen Tip O'Neill and Edward Kennedy. Together they convinced promoter Bob Arum to get a title shot for a kid from Brockton who had only two losses on his record and so many bloody wins that no one with a title belt would fight him.

"I didn't know much about him, but I put him on a card in Monte Carlo against a guy named Norberto Cabrera

He attacked Hearns ... pounding him to the floor to bring the fight to a conclusion, with Hearns unclear who he was or why this bald guy was hitting him.

underneath an Antuofermo title fight," Arum recalled. "After Marvin was finished, all the crowd was talking about was him. That's when I thought he would be great."

That's how it turned out, although it took a while longer than Arum expected, because his new middleweight fought a controversial draw with Antuofermo five months later and did not manage to win the title for another year. He finally did it against Alan Minter on Sept. 27, 1980.

Hagler would defend his title 12 times before losing a disputed decision to the elusive Sugar Ray Leonard on April 6, 1987, a night that so disgusted him that he retired from boxing and never came back. "How can they say you lost when you weren't even in a fight?" Hagler reportedly asked a friend that night.

No man could sustain forever Hagler's level of commitment to training and the spartan life he felt was necessary to "go to war," but at its peak no one could survive in the face of it. Even Hearns, who would win world titles in five weight classes, could not go the distance in the 1985 fight that was Hagler's finest moment.

"That was the greatest eight minutes of boxing I've ever seen in 28 years in the game," Arum marveled.

Blood streaming down his face from a gash above his eye, Hagler simply would not be denied in the third round. He attacked Hearns and destroyed his will to stand, pounding him to the floor to bring the fight to a conclusion with Hearns unclear who he was or why this bald guy was hitting him. ❖

Above: Blood streaming down his face from a gash above his eye, Hagler still managed to hold his own against Hearns, and ultimately he showed that he would not be denied.

Q. Many times we have heard the quote, "It ain't over till the fat lady sings." Who really said it the first time? Was it in reference to Kate Smith?

V.A., MIDDLETOWN, R.I.

A. Believed to be a modern version of the proverb, "Don't count your chickens until they're hatched," the phrase has been around for years but no one seems able to pinpoint the source. Though it echoes a famous Yogi Berra-ism, researchers more often attribute the "fat lady" saying to San Antonio sports editor Dan Cook. In the mid-1970s, it was seen or heard several times during newspaper and broadcast coverage of baseball's World Series and there appears to be a basketball connection, as well. A widely shared view is that it has something to do with operas that end in arias by well-built divas, and/or it may specifically reference Kate Smith, the generously proportioned performer who sang "God Bless America" at the conclusion of political party conventions and World Series games in the '30s and '40s. Other popular versions of the phrase include "Church ain't out till the fat lady sings" and "The game's not over until the last man strikes out."

40 more thrillers

JULY 25, 2004 ›› BY MARC CARIG, GLOBE CORRESPONDENT

FENWAY 2004: FIREWORKS AND FISTICUFFS

Bill **Mueller looked on with everyone else as Red Sox teammates Manny** Ramirez and Trot Nixon sent a couple of late-inning blasts sailing toward the bleachers, only to see a heavy wind reduce them to outs. The Red Sox still trailed by two in the ninth, and Mueller had no way of knowing that he was about to put the finishing touch on what might be the greatest regular-season game in Fenway Park's rich history — an 11-10 victory over the Yankees.

All he knew when he stepped into the batter's box was that the dust had barely settled from a much earlier, benches-clearing melee triggered by a violent tussle between Sox stalwart Jason Varitek and Yankees star Alex Rodriguez. It was that kind of game. Explosive.

The brawl erupted in the third after pitcher Bronson Arroyo plunked Rodriguez in the left arm with the Yankees already leading 3-0.

First, Rodriguez spewed a stream of invectives toward the mound as Varitek stood between him and his pitcher. Then the catcher brusquely advised the Yankee star to stop yapping and take first base. The two exchanged words of their own before Varitek attempted to feed Rodriguez his catcher's mitt. The fight was on and players raced from both dugouts to join what soon became a typical baseball brouhaha. Varitek, Rodriguez and a few others were eventually ejected.

The brawl gave the Red Sox a temporary boost, but it seemed all would be for naught when the ninth inning rolled around. The Ramirez and Nixon long flies were the reason Mueller wasn't terribly ambitious when he stepped into the batter's box against Yankee super-closer Mariano Rivera, who had converted 23 straight save opportunities heading into the game.

"I'm just trying to get in a good hitter's count and have a good at-bat," Mueller recalled later. "See some pitches, get on base..."

In other words, he would have been content to advance pinch-runner David McCarty. Getting on base would have been a bonus, and slamming a home run wasn't even a consideration.

"Not even close," Mueller admitted.

But Mueller blew away his own expectations with a two-run, walkoff homer to help the Red Sox strike back at the Empire. A Yankee lead that had grown to 9-4 in the middle of the game was finally obliterated.

Kevin Millar had ignited the final rally by slapping an RBI single to right-center (driving in Nomar Garciaparra, who had doubled) before giving way to McCarty. The homer that followed sent the sellout crowd into a frenzy and Mueller's teammates sprinting onto the field, including the ones banished to the clubhouse for brawling.

"My head almost hit the ceiling in the locker room," said Varitek. After witnessing the blast on television in the clubhouse, ejected manager Terry Francona raced down the stairs, through a tunnel, and onto the field — barefoot.

Finally, the game gave the Red Sox a new theme song. After Garciaparra's two-run single in the fourth inning, a prophetic lyric from Chumbawamba's "Tubthumping" was heard over the Fenway sound system: "I get knocked down but I get up again, you're never gonna keep me down." ❖

Bob Hohler, Globe Staff, contributed to this report.

Baseball

WHO	**RED SOX** VS. **YANKEES.**
WHERE	**FENWAY PARK,** BOSTON.
WHEN	**JULY 24, 2004.**
WHY THE DRAMA	Not only a walkoff blast, but also a benches-clearing brawl. Playoff intensity in July. Only in Boston.

	R	H	E
YANKEES	10	12	0
RED SOX	11	15	4

The season that had it all

The 2004 season will go down as the greatest of them all, a 162-game roller coaster that twisted, turned, and spiraled Red Sox Nation into a triumphant frenzy. There were trials and tribulations, hellos and goodbyes, bloody socks and Papi power... Oh yes, and Manny being Manny.

In Theo we trusted as Red Sox management placed a renewed emphasis on pitching and defense. We bid adieu to the omni-popular Nomar Garciaparra and welcomed defensive wizard Orlando Cabrera.

We marveled in the greatness of Pedro Martinez and Curt Schilling. We saw Keith Foulke bring stability to a bullpen that was always in disarray. We basked in the glory of Mr. Clutch, David Ortiz. We saw our fearless captain (Jason Varitek) go toe-to-toe with our ultimate enemy (A-Rod).

It was a season that erased the myths of curses and the drawn-out playoff tragedies of yesteryear. It was the greatest season of all time, one that cannot be duplicated, no matter how many more memories these heart-stopping Red Sox give us.

Above: Bill Mueller's walkoff homer in the ninth turned out to be a sign of things to come for Yankees closer Mariano Rivera.

ORTIZ BLASTS OFF

OCTOBER 9, 2004 » BY DAN SHAUGHNESSY, GLOBE STAFF

*I*n one of the most electrifying moments in the history of a ballpark that's almost older than household electricity, slugger David Ortiz propelled the wild-and-crazy Red Sox to the second round of the 2004 playoffs with a 10th-inning, first-pitch, two-out, two-run, walk-off homer into the seats above Fenway Park's left-field wall.

Big Papi's mighty clout, struck under Friday night lights at 8:21, beat the Anaheim Angels, 8-6. The blast, off a juicy Jarrod Washburn slider, powered the Sox to a stunning American League Division Series sweep, only their second in 20 postseason series since 1903.

"We're just the idiots this year," Johnny Damon had declared prior to Game 1. "We feel like we have to have fun."

The Carlton Fisk-like Monster Mash also triggered yet another Delta-house, champagne-soaked celebration in the Boston locker room, on the field, in the stands, and in the streets around the ancient ballyard.

"He just made a mistake," said Ortiz when asked about the pitch he hit. "He gave me a slider that was up. Kind of high... a pitch I could hit."

Ortiz was still wearing his glare-preventive eyeblack when he stepped to the plate 4 hours 11 minutes after the game started. Darkness had fallen around Fenway and so had the mood in the stands after the Angels bounced back from a 6-1 deficit with five runs in the top of the seventh inning. Vladimir Guerrero's grand slam tied the game and threw a scare into Red Sox Nation. No Boston team had ever blown a lead of more than five runs in a postseason game.

But Keith Foulke righted the ship with an inning and a third of shutout relief and then the much-maligned Derek Lowe made his first relief appearance of the season in the 10th. Lowe put runners on first and third with two outs, but got series goat Chone Figgins to ground out on a nice play by shortstop Orlando Cabrera.

In the bottom half, after ace reliever Francisco Rodriguez fanned Manny Ramirez for the second out, Angels manager Mike Scioscia summoned Game 1 starter Washburn. Ortiz turned on his first pitch.

The Boston dugout emptied in record time while the bear-like Ortiz circled the bases. After pinch runner Pokey Reese crossed the plate, Ortiz lumbered around third and was engulfed by his teammates at home plate. The ensuing celebration featured Kevin Millar and Lowe leading a parade of champagne-spraying Sox back onto the field. Almost an hour after the game, Trot Nixon and Gabe Kapler rewarded the stragglers, grabbing a microphone and thanking fans on behalf of their teammates. It seemed no one wanted to go home.

Few expected the Red Sox to win the series in straight sets, but they did. Playing on the road, the Sox beat the Angels, 9-3 and 8-3 in the first two games — in other words, not much drama. But Game 3 more than made up for it. ❖

For what happened after this (as if you didn't know), see page 14.

Above: David Ortiz made a regular habit of causing mob scenes at home plate in 2004. This one came after he hit the 10th-inning homer in Game 3 of the Angels-Red Sox playoff series.
Left: Ortiz enjoyed his late-inning trips around the bases every bit as much as the Fenway faithful did.

THE IMPOSSIBLE DREAM TEAM

I **buy the tickets on a whim.**
It's a lunch-hour purchase in late July of 1967. Flush with cash on a summer job payday, I hustle down to Fenway Park, hoping to scoop decent tickets for some upcoming Red Sox games. I had begun the baseball season as a typically blase transplant from Joisey, but now I am swept up in what remains the greatest fan experience of my life.

Right: A celebratory shower always seemed like a fun idea back in '67.
Below: Safe at home? Carl Yastrzemski's Red Sox used Fenway to great advantage in their game against the Twins. But they went on to lose Game 7 of the World Series in Boston.

"Gimme some for Detroit," I say. "Ooo, how about that twinighter with KC? The Senators? Sure. California? Why not?" And then, one last inspiration.

"Minnesota's here on the last day of the season? Hey, ya never know. Two for Oct. 1, please."

Two tickets. Six bucks. Section 22, Box 133E, Seats 9 and 10. Behind the screen on the last day of the season. I hope it means something. Miraculously, it does.

By Oct. 1, what had been the greatest four-team pennant race in American League history has been reduced to three teams with Chicago's elimination. It has come to this: The Red Sox-Twins winner is guaranteed at least a tie, and will win the pennant if Detroit can't take two from California in these glorious pre-playoff days.

Sox manager Dick Williams has Jim Lonborg and his 21-9 record ready on three days rest. But Twins manager Cal Ermer has Dean Chance, and not only has he won 20, he's 4-1 against Boston while Lonborg is 0-3 against Minnesota.

The Twins take a 2-0 lead into the sixth. Lonborg is leading off. He bunts down the third-base line, and Cesar Tovar can't make the play.

The rest of the inning is a jumble of images. I see Rod Carew diving for, and narrowly missing, Jerry Adair's shot up the middle. First and second. Dalton Jones slaps one through the shortstop/third-base hole. Now the bases are loaded and Yaz is up. Perhaps never in my life have I more deeply connected with the word "faith." Normally a pessimist, I know that Carl Yastrzemski, having been a continual hero for 161 games, will get one more desperately needed hit. He buzzes Chance's left ear with a line drive to center for a two-run, game-tying single.

The Minnesota horror is just beginning. Hawk Harrelson chops one to short. Zoilo Versalles has only one play — to first. He throws home instead. The go-ahead run scores.

Al Worthington replaces Chance. Bad move. A wild pitch moves the runners up. A second wild pitch scores Yaz. 4-2. George Scott fans. But Rico Petrocelli walks, and Reggie Smith hits a wicked short-hopper off Harmon Killebrew's knee at first, driving in the fifth run.

Five runs in. Can Lonnie hold the lead?

Yes, thanks to Yaz. Killebrew is on third and Oliva on first with two away in the eighth, when Bob Allison rifles one into the left-field corner. Killebrew scores and Oliva makes it into third easily, but Allison overplays his hand. He's going to challenge Yastrzemski's arm. This is not a smart thing to do in 1967. Allison is tagged before he reaches the bag, and instead of men on first (or second) and third with two away and Lonnie staggering, the inning — and season — are over for the Minnesota Twins.

Rich Rollins pops meekly to Rico for the final out of the ninth, and now delirious fans are carrying Jim Lonborg off the field.

On my Green Line ride home, transistor radios blare out Ernie Harwell's call of the second Detroit-California game, and when Don Mincher swats a homer for the Angels, the entire streetcar cheers. Later, Dick McAuliffe grounds into a game-ending double play, giving the 1967 American League pennant to the 100-to-1 shot, the Boston Red Sox ❖

Baseball

FINAL GAME OF THE REGULAR SEASON

WHO	**RED SOX** VS **TWINS.**
WHERE	**FENWAY PARK,** BOSTON.
WHEN	**OCTOBER 1, 1967.**
WHY THE DRAMA	The last game of the year, tied with the Twins, winner take all.

	R	H	E
TWINS	3	7	1
RED SOX	5	12	2

What Happened Next

Cinderella drops the ball

As we know, the Red Sox ultimately came up short in the 1967 World Series, losing Game 7 to the St. Louis Cardinals at Fenway Park. Sox pitcher Jim Lonborg, working on two days rest, couldn't quite match the wizardry of Bob Gibson, who spun his third complete-game victory of the Series (his ERA in those games was 1.00) in a 7-2 win. Fans were disappointed, but in a strange way the Series had been anticlimactic anyway, given the theatrics staged during the regular season. Those who lived through that mystical baseball season know that it remains the yardstick by which improbable team dramas are measured.

FISK'S FENWAY MOMENT HANGS WITH THE BEST

*A*nd all of a sudden the ball was there, like Boston's Mystic River Bridge, suspended out in the black of the morning.

When it finally crashed off the mesh attached to the Fenway Park left-field foul pole, one step after another the reaction unfurled: from Carlton Fisk's convulsive leap to John Kiley's booming of the "Hallelujah Chorus" to the wearing off of numbness to the outcry that echoed all across the cold New England countryside.

At 12:34 a.m., Fisk's epic, 12th-inning home run brought a 7-6 end to Game 6 of the 1975 World Series, a game that will be the pride of historians in the year 2525, a game won and lost what seemed like a dozen times, and a game that brings back summertime one more day.

For this game to end so swiftly, so definitively, was the fitting final turn. An inning before, there had been a Dwight Evans catch that Sparky Anderson claimed was as great as he's ever seen. In the ninth, George Foster's throw ruined a bases-loaded, none-out certain victory for the Red Sox. In the eighth, there was a dramatic, pinch-hit three-run homer by Bernie Carbo as the obituaries were being prepared. And there was the downfall of pitcher Luis Tiant, who couldn't keep the lid on, despite Fred Lynn's three-run, first-inning homer.

Finally Fisk put the exclamation mark at the end of what he called "the most emotional game I've ever played in." The home run came off Pat Darcy and made a winner of Rick Wise, who had become the record 12th pitcher in this 241-minute civil war that seemed to last closer to four score and seven years.

But the place one must begin is the bottom of the eighth, Cincinnati leading, 6-3, and the end so clear. El Tiante had left in the top of the inning to what apparently was to be the last of his 1975 ovations; he who had become the conquering king had been found to be just a man, and it seemed so certain. Autumn had been postponed for the last time.

Out came an implausible hero to a two-out, two-on situation against Rawlins J. Eastwick III, and just like that Carbo sent a line drive into the center-field bleachers. What had been a lachrymose scene had become mad, sensuous Fenway again.

In the top of the 11th, the Reds had it taken away from them again, this time by Dwight Evans. With Ken Griffey at first and one out, Joe Morgan crashed a line drive toward the seats in right. Evans made his racing, web-of-the-glove, staggering catch as he crossed the warning track ("It would have been two rows in," said Reds bullpen catcher Bill Plummer) and then heaved the ball to first for the double play.

The Reds did not score in the top of the 12th against Wise, setting the stage for Fisk's unforgettable swat. ❖

Left: There really was no place like home for New Hampshire boy Carlton Fisk, especially in the 12th-inning of a classic Game 6 at Fenway Park.

WHO	RED SOX VS. REDS.
WHERE	FENWAY PARK, BOSTON.
WHEN	OCTOBER 21, 1975.
WHY THE DRAMA	With the unwavering Fenway faithful in need of a miracle, Pudge sent a majestic shot into the Boston night. But would it stay fair?

GAME 1, OCTOBER 11	R	H	E
REDS	0	5	0
RED SOX	6	12	0

GAME 2, OCTOBER 12	R	H	E
REDS	3	7	1
RED SOX	2	7	0

GAME 3, OCTOBER 14	R	H	E
RED SOX	5	10	2
REDS	6	7	0

GAME 4, OCTOBER 15	R	H	E
RED SOX	5	11	1
REDS	4	9	1

GAME 5, OCTOBER 16	R	H	E
RED SOX	2	5	0
REDS	6	8	0

GAME 6, OCTOBER 21	R	H	E
REDS	6	14	0
RED SOX	7	10	1

GAME 7, OCTOBER 22	R	H	E
REDS	4	9	0
RED SOX	3	5	2

Above: The walkoff began as a swat towards left field.

THE PERFECT WAVE

JULY 23, 2000 »» BY DAN SHAUGHNESSY, GLOBE STAFF

Pat Darcy had cruised through the bottom halves of the 10th and 11th frames, twice retiring the side in order, six up and six down. In the dugout Carlton Fisk, due to lead off, removed his catcher's gear and looked for a bat. He had been walked intentionally in his prior plate appearance and was tiring. His bat felt heavy. He asked shortstop Rick Burleson if he could use his bat, which was lighter.

Fred Lynn, the rookie who was later honored as the American League Most Valuable Player for 1975, was due up second. He was already in the on-deck circle when Fisk came out. His fatigue had lifted. He felt a change in the midnight air which had been hazy most of the night but now it felt clear and fresh. Fisk said to Lynn, "Freddie, I can feel something good. I'm gonna hit one off the Wall. Drive me in."

"Sounds good to me," said Lynn.

More than 60 million people were tuned in to NBC's telecast and as Fisk stretched in the batter's box, a TV graphic revealed he was 5 for 21 in the Series thus far. Darcy's first pitch was outside.

The next one was down and rode inside. Fisk, a dead pull hitter, made his living on pitches like this. When the

Above: Fisk gave the ball plenty of encouragement to stay fair.
Right: Years later, he came back to Fenway for an official renaming of the left-field foul pole in his honor.

ball left Darcy's hand, Fisk knew it was going to be a pitch he could hit. With a nice uppercut swing that even Ted Williams would envy, Fisk swung and got the barrel of the bat on the ball. Fisk immediately knew he had gotten plenty of wood on it. He knew the trajectory was good. But given his bat speed and the location of the pitch, the ball seemed destined to hook foul.

Fisk started down the line, carrying Burleson's bat the first few steps. He dropped the bat and started to yell at the ball, "Stay fair! Stay fair!" He never actually ran. He skipped sideways, watching the ball, then began waving his arms from left to right.

Soaring into hardball history, the ball clanged off the pole and caromed directly into Foster's glove. Foster flipped the ball into his other hand and examined it briefly as Fenway rocked on its 1912 foundation. ❖

The boy next door

Growing up in New England will always get you extra points with Red Sox fans, and Carlton Fisk is a Yankee (the good kind) through and through. After attending the University of New Hampshire, that state's favorite son was picked in the first round of the 1967 amateur draft by the Red Sox. He made a swift impact, racking up historic numbers for a catcher.

Best known for his epic Game 6 homer that nailed the left field foul pole in the '75 Series, Fisk retired as the all-time home-run leader at his position. That left field post was properly renamed "The Fisk Pole," and Pudge was inducted into the MLB Hall of Fame in 2000.

Yes, we know that the Carbo homer was more important. But thanks to unending video replays, the Fisk shot is the one that everybody remembers. It revived baseball.

A PESKY DEBATE AND A MAD DASH

In the eighth inning of one of the great Game 7s of all time, Enos "Country" Slaughter dashed into World Series lore and Red Sox Nation infamy. With the score tied 3-3 in the finale of an epic 1946 series that pitted Ted Williams' Sox against Stan Musial's Cards, the fiery Slaughter had led off with a single and was still on first base with two outs. As Sox hurler Bob Klinger wound up and released his pitch to the Cardinals' Harry Walker, Slaughter took off to steal second base. He never stopped.

Walker blooped a rather innocent-looking hit to center field. Substitute center fielder Leon Culberson's relay throw came to shortstop Johnny Pesky, who turned and was shocked to find Slaughter already rounding third base and heading for home. Pesky hesitated slightly — how "slightly" has been the grist for debate among Red Sox fans for decades. His throw home was late and off target and the Cardinals went ahead, 4-3, a lead they would not give up in the ninth.

Slaughter's audacity gave the Cardinals a world championship and the Red Sox their first World Series defeat. It also gave the chroniclers of the Sox faithful an infamous intonation: "Pesky held the ball."

Some say that play alone was Slaughter's ticket to the Hall of Fame.

"That still burns my butt today. It's absurd," Slaughter said in an interview with the St. Louis Post-Dispatch in 1996. "You look at my stats sheet. I think my stats speak for themselves."

Slaughter had warmed up for his seventh-game heroics with four hits in Game 4, during which he used his legendary throwing arm to turn an apparent run-scoring fly into a putout at the plate, where a surprised Rudy York was called out. When the amazed Boston reporters cornered Slaughter about the play after the game, he growled, "What the hell? Don't they run in the American League?"

During the next game, Slaughter was struck by a pitch on the right elbow. Fearing a blood clot that could endanger Slaughter's life, the Cardinals' doctor urged him to hang up his spikes and watch the rest of the Series.

Above: While Johnny Pesky may or may not have been asleep at short-stop, Enos Slaughter motored right past third base and never stopped until he'd slid in safely with the back-breaking run.

Baseball

WHO	**RED SOX** VS **CARDINALS.**
WHERE	**SPORTSMAN'S PARK,** ST. LOUIS.
WHEN	**OCTOBER 15, 1946.**
WHY THE DRAMA	Did Johnny Pesky hold the ball? It's the question that has haunted his entire Boston career, and this is a guy we like.

	R	H	E
GAME 1 / OCTOBER 6			
RED SOX	3	9	2
CARDINALS	2	7	0
GAME 2 / OCTOBER 7			
RED SOX	0	4	1
CARDINALS	3	6	0
GAME 3 / OCTOBER 9			
CARDINALS	0	6	1
RED SOX	4	8	0
GAME 4 / OCTOBER 10			
CARDINALS	12	20	1
RED SOX	3	9	4
GAME 5 / OCTOBER 11			
CARDINALS	3	4	1
RED SOX	6	11	3
GAME 6 / OCTOBER 13			
RED SOX	1	7	0
CARDINALS	4	8	0
GAME 7 / OCTOBER 15			
RED SOX	3	8	0
CARDINALS	4	9	1

Known for his short, just-fair home runs, Johnny Pesky will be forever immortalized by the right field foul post at Fenway Park, dubbed Pesky's Pole in his honor. Pesky received a 2004 World Series championship ring for his contributions to the organization as a player, manager, and coach. It had only taken the Sox 58 years to reverse his personal curse, finally taking four straight games from the Cardinals faster than fans could say "mad dash."

Said "Country" without hesitation, "It's my life, Doc, I'll play." And the stage was set for what came to be known as "The Mad Dash."

"I have young guys ask me about that play who hadn't even been born in 1946," Pesky told The Boston Globe, recalling the series in a 1979 interview.

"I was going to cover second, because Slaughter was stealing. I was starting toward second and Walker hit the ball to left-center... I got the ball and, when I turned, there was a little hitch and maybe that's what people saw.

"I don't know. I just know that when I turned around, Slaughter was about 22 feet away from the plate, and the only way I could have stopped him was with a rifle. Shot him."

Slaughter beat the throw home by 3 feet. ❖

HENDU MAGIC

He is part of Boston folklore, no less than Honey Fitz, Arthur Fiedler or Johnny Kelley. He is David Henderson, an otherwise anonymous ex-baseball player who launched the Missiles of October in the infamous autumn of 1986.

That was the season fuzzy-faced Roger Clemens went 24-4, Oil Can Boyd quit the Red Sox in midseason and, eventually, Mookie Wilson hit a slow roller down the first base line.

Hendu is the man who came within one strike of getting his own statue in downtown Boston. Sam Adams, James Michael Curley, David Henderson. It almost happened.

For citizens of Red Sox Nation, the sight of Henderson conjures memories of the biggest miracle of '86, the one where a benchwarmer from Seattle lived out a two-week Faustian fantasy and brought the star-crossed Sox to the brink.

Hendu forever reminds us of the best of '86. Clemens wasn't just Cy Young, he was MVP. Jim Rice had his last 20-homer, 100-RBI season, and Wade Boggs of course won the batting title. But it was Henderson who carried the Red Sox in the postseason.

A brief recap for those of you who missed the most dramatic three weeks of playoff baseball in the history of the sport: In the American League Championship Series, the Red Sox trailed the California Angels, 5-2, in the ninth inning of Game 5. California led the best-of-seven series, 3-1, and Reggie Jackson was hugging Gene Mauch on the top step of the Angel dugout as the Sox started to go down in the ninth. Don Baylor's two-run homer cut the margin to 5-4, and then with two out and one on, Henderson stepped in to face Donnie Moore. Hendu smacked a homer and the Red Sox went on to win it in extra innings on a — what else? — Henderson sacrifice fly.

Two weeks later, with the Red Sox leading the Mets, three games to two, and tied, 3-3, in the top of the 10th inning of World Series Game 6, Henderson cracked a solo homer off the Mets' Rick Aguilera. The hardball universe prepared for the merciful end of the Curse of the Bambino . . . and then came the most hideous, heinous collapse in sports history. And Dave Henderson became a footnote, a trivia answer. He became the man who almost shot Liberty Valance.

Henderson conjures memories of the biggest miracle of '86, the one where a benchwarmer from Seattle brought the star-crossed Sox to the brink.

Many lives were altered by the 1986 postseason. California's Moore — who threw the gopher ball to Hendu in the ALCS — was never the same and eventually shot his wife, then killed himself with a handgun. Moore's agent and teammates claimed the hurler was unable to cope with the trauma of having surrendered the crushing home run. The Mets' Aguilera, Henderson's victim in the World Series, went on to become a relief ace and wound up pitching for the 1995 Red Sox. It was Aguilera who coughed up the crucial homer to Albert Belle in the first round of the playoffs.

Henderson's Game 5 homer was his only hit of the ALCS, but it was the start of a well-timed hot streak. He hit .400 in the World Series. ❖

Above: Dave Henderson got a big hand on his way in after he homered in the ninth.

Baseball

WHO	**RED SOX** VS **ANGELS.**
WHERE	**ANAHEIM STADIUM,** ANAHEIM.
WHEN	**OCTOBER 12, 1986.**
WHY THE DRAMA	The stage was set for an Angels/Mets World Series, but Hendu and the Red Sox had other plans.

GAME 1 / OCTOBER 7	R	H	E
ANGELS	8	11	0
RED SOX	1	5	1

GAME / OCTOBER 8	R	H	E
ANGELS	2	11	3
RED SOX	9	13	2

GAME 3 / OCTOBER 10	R	H	E
RED SOX	3	9	1
ANGELS	5	8	0

GAME 4 / OCTOBER 11	R	H	E
RED SOX	3	6	1
ANGELS	4	11	2

GAME 5 / OCTOBER 12	R	H	E
RED SOX	7	12	0
ANGELS	6	13	0

GAME 6 / OCTOBER 14	R	H	E
ANGELS	4	11	1
RED SOX	10	16	1

GAME 7 / OCTOBER 16	R	H	E
ANGELS	1	6	2
RED SOX	8	8	1

Nice move

Red Sox GM Lou Gorman brought David Henderson to Boston in a trade earlier in the year, and boy did it pay off. Hendu's late-inning heroics in Game 5 brought Anaheim Stadium to its knees. The final two games of the series were a mere formality; BoSox fans swooned as the home team beat up on its West Coast guests. The Sox were headed to another ill-fated World Series and the hub had a fresh hero to applaud. Not bad for the new kid on the block.

THE SINGLE MOST INFAMOUS ERROR

When Bill Buckner strode to the bar at Murphy's Seafood and Steakhouse in Boise, Idaho, on a crisp October Saturday afternoon, nobody noticed. The half-dozen televisions around the room were all tuned to soccer and football and the bartender had to be asked to change the station to that day's Red Sox-Yankees American League Championship Series game, a classic Roger Clemens-Pedro Martinez matchup at Fenway. But even when the game went up on a screen it was as ignored as a moldy potato by the pregame Boise State football crowd, all dressed in Day-Glo orange for the homecoming game against Tulsa.

With the Red Sox again tantalizingly close to the World Series and the championship that had eluded them since 1918 (and would soon do so again), Buckner had consented, reluctantly, to a 10-minute interview at his 5-acre mountain home. Also planned was a photograph of him in his trophy room. But then the trophy room shot and the home visit were vetoed by Buckner's wife, Jody. She was sick of the press who still harped on Buckner's error on the routine ground ball that skipped between his legs and gave the Mets the Game 6 victory over the Red Sox in the 1986 World Series to tie the series. In Game 7, the Sox blew an early lead and lost despite Buckner's two hits. Jody had good reason to be angry. A reporter once called the house to inquire if Bill was contemplating suicide.

When the interview began, it quickly became clear that if Buckner was bearing any demons 17 years later, he hid them well. He was relaxed, smiling and sociable. Nor was he living in his own private Idaho, 2,200 miles from Boston. "No, I'm not in exile," he said. "I bought a ranch here in the '70s. I planned on moving here then. I just didn't have the opportunity."

Right: Bill Buckner's mishandling of a routine ground ball opened the door just enough for the Mets, who went on to take the 1986 World Series title in seven games.

Baseball

WHO	**RED SOX** VS **METS.**	
WHERE	**SHEA STADIUM,** NEW YORK.	
WHEN	**OCTOBER 25, 1986.**	
WHY THE DRAMA	Two strikes, two outs, three separate times… How could it come to this?	

Sorry. We know this one hurts. We know it's negative. But it's still the one. Buckner's play is not the reason the Red Sox lost the World Series, but it's the symbolic, defining moment for the region's most important sports team. We defy you to find a New Englander over age 30 who can't remember this event.

GAME 1 / OCTOBER 18	R	H	E
RED SOX	1	5	0
METS	0	4	1

GAME 2 / OCTOBER 19	R	H	E
RED SOX	9	18	0
METS	3	8	1

GAME 3 / OCTOBER 21	R	H	E
METS	7	13	0
RED SOX	1	5	0

GAME 4 / OCTOBER 22	R	H	E
METS	6	12	0
RED SOX	2	7	1

GAME 5 / OCTOBER 23	R	H	E
METS	2	10	1
RED SOX	4	12	0

GAME 6 / OCTOBER 25	R	H	E
RED SOX	5	13	3
METS	6	8	2

GAME 7 / OCTOBER 27	R	H	E
RED SOX	5	9	0
METS	8	10	0

Billy Buck was amicable and forthright, comfortable in his own skin. He was also fit and youthful for a guy in his 50s — no stomach, no gray, and no limp.

"I got a great life," he said. "I like the way things are going. I don't sit in the woods and think about it. Ever."

The ground ball in question, off the bat of the Mets' Mookie Wilson, went skip, skip, and scoot. The play was over in a couple seconds, but its aftermath went on seemingly forever. A whole generation reached the age of consent learning about the error through grainy, black-and-white photos and replays every October at World Series time. It's been called the Zapruder film of baseball. Buckner never thought the miscue would take on a life of its own and make him the poster boy for the Curse of the Bambino.

"It's unbelievable," said the first baseman who played in four decades for four teams other than the Red Sox and accrued 2,715 hits. "You know what? This is the honest-to-God's truth. My first thought was, 'Oh [expletive], we lost the game.' The second thought was, 'Oh man, we get to play the seventh game of the World Series.' I mean, I was having so much fun. There was no doubt in my mind we were going to win the last game."

Despite so many games during so many years in baseball, Buckner remembered all the details of that singular Game 6 sequence. "I had a bad feeling about [the Mets rally]," he said. "I mean, we had the game wrapped up and then all of a sudden it's tied, and the other team has momentum.

"The whole play was bizarre. Marty Barrett was standing on second base to try and pick off Ray Knight. We had him picked off. I saw Marty move over to second, so I moved way over toward the hole. Normally with Mookie, you would play up with a runner on second base. You play a little deeper because you don't want the ball to go through. So then he dribbled the ball down the first base line. The reason he would've beat it out had nothing to do with Stanley getting over there. It's because I was so far out of position, trying to cover the hole over there. An infield hit still would've had Knight on third base. I had run up a long way, but I don't remember feeling like I was rushed.

"I didn't feel any kind of tension to catch the ground ball. Usually, when you miss a ground ball, it's because you look up. I didn't look up. The ball hit . . . I'm pretty sure the ball hit something . . . because the ball didn't go underneath my glove. It went to the right of my glove. It took a little bit of a funny hop, bounced to the right a little bit. It wasn't like, you know, you feel rushed and you look up. It took a funny hop. I mean, it's funny. It's funny. What do I chalk it up to? Fate. That's part of the game."

Even decades later, Buckner noted that he still hears "stuff."

"I laugh at it," he said. "Sports are for teaching young people to deal with success and failure. ... I hope the kids in Boston aren't taught that if you make a mistake, all the good things you've done all your life go out the window.

"I didn't lose the World Series," he said. "Everyone knows one play doesn't decide a seven-game series."

And he's maintained perspective. "Was that the worst moment of my life? No. My dad passing away when I was 14," he said.

As for good times, Buckner remembered one in particular. "The people of Boston gave me that standing ovation when I made the team in 1990."

The Sox released Buckner midway through the 1987 season. He played for the California Angels and the Kansas City Royals before returning for 22 games in 1990 in Boston at the age of 41.

"That was probably my biggest accomplishment. [Sox manager Joe] Morgan didn't want me on there, but I hit the hell out of the ball in spring training. He had no choice," explained Buckner. "Then that ovation from the [opening-day Fenway Park] crowd. How cool was that? It brought tears to my eyes." ❖

Left: The Sox first baseman was the picture of dejection in the dugout. Below: Years later, though, Buckner could smile about it all as he sat in an Idaho bar thinking back to his days in a Boston uniform.

What Happened Next

Sins of the past

JUNE 28, 2006

BY CHRIS SNOW, GLOBE STAFF

Among the sounds that rippled through Fenway Park were claps and whistles and other such indications of appreciation and pride, and, so it seemed, no audible dissatisfaction. Such was the greeting as the name "Mr. Bill Buckner" scrolled across the stadium video board and poured through the Fenway speaker system during a 20th anniversary ceremony honoring the 1986 edition of the Red Sox.

"There wasn't one boo. That was great, wasn't it?" said Oil Can Boyd, one of several members of the '86 team on the field before the start of a game against the New York Mets. "That shows the class of the Boston fans, showing him some love.

"That was just a moment in time," Boyd said of the ball that beat Buckner through the wickets in Game 6 of the '86 World Series. "People keep reminiscing about that. It doesn't just hurt Buck, it hurts us all. We all lost that game and that Series."

Unfortunately, it was Buckner who took the fall.

Boston's most famous scapegoat couldn't be on hand to hear the Fenway faithful applaud him in 2006, but several of his former Red Sox teammates were, and many were grateful for the reception he and they received.

"I wish he was here. Because we would have never, ever come as close to the World Series without Billy Buckner and the way he performed in '86," said Wade Boggs.

Some of Buckner's numbers in 1986: 153 games, .267 average, 39 doubles, 18 HRs, 102 RBIs. His RBI total ranked 10th in the league. He fanned just 25 times in 629 at-bats, making him baseball's hardest strikeout that year (once every 25.2 at-bats).

Maybe Red Sox Nation is finally ready to remember it all.

THE CURSED ONE, BUCKY DENT

"**ey Dan, this is B.F. Dent from Florida calling.**"That's the message Bucky Dent left on my office voice mail many years after he broke the Nation's heart in a one-game playoff at the end of the 1978 regular season. I've played it for about a thousand people.

Here's a clue for you all: Bucky's middle name is not Fred. It's Earl. He was born in Savannah, Ga., in 1951 and on a fateful October Monday he hit the home run that still inspires Red Sox fans to curse his very existence.

Bucky (Bleeping) Dent — he hit a home run for the ages and got a new middle name out of the deal.

On the day in question, the Yankees and Red Sox faced off at Fenway for the AL East crown. Boston had come back to tie for the lead on the final day of the season, after blowing a 6 1/2-game lead entering September.

But what could have been the icing on a dream season turned into a nightmare for Red Sox fans when light-hitting Yankees shortstop Bucky Dent lofted his three-run homer just over the Green Monster in the seventh inning to erase the Boston lead for good.

Earlier, Carl Yastrzemski started the scoring by smashing an 0-and-1 Ron Guidry fastball into the stands down the right-field line leading off the second for a 1-0 lead. The lead doubled when Rick Burleson doubled, Jerry Remy bunted him to third and Jim Rice singled. A bid for more was squelched when, with two runners aboard, New York's Lou Piniella made a nice running catch of a Fred Lynn drive to the right field corner.

Mike Torrez entered the top of the seventh riding a two-hitter and the 2-0 lead. Chris Chambliss and Roy White both stroked one-out singles, and one out later Dent came to the plate. After fouling a ball off his foot, he switched to a Mickey Rivers bat (Rivers, who was on deck, noticed Dent's bat had a chip in it). With a 1-1 count, Dent turned on an inside pitch and, aided by a wind that earlier in the game had been blowing in, just cleared the wall down the left-field line for a 3-2 Yankees lead.

Left and right: Bucky Dent's crushing home run made many Red Sox fans swear off believing in the dream ever again. That resolution lasted about six months.

Baseball

WHO	**RED SOX** VS. **YANKEES.**
WHERE	**FENWAY PARK,** BOSTON.
WHEN	**OCTOBER 2, 1978.**
WHY THE DRAMA	It was baseball's Game of the Century. New York-Boston. Tied after 162 games. And Bucky Dent's cap-pistol homer is the one we take to our graves.

	R	H	E
YANKEES	5	8	0
RED SOX	4	11	0

The suspense of the 1978 Red Sox season started long before most households in New England ever heard the name Bucky Dent. In mid-July, the Sox were cruising along with a seemingly Yankee-proof 14-game lead in the AL East. But as history has shown us, Boston baseball is never a simple mathematical calculation. Slowly but surely, the Sox lead slipped to where the whole season rested on this epic, one-game playoff at Fenway. We all know how it ended, but we typically forget the extended trauma that preceded Dent's final blow to the heart.

A Thurman Munson RBI double off reliever Bob Stanley and Reggie Jackson's solo home run made it 5-2 before the Red Sox rallied. They cut the lead to 5-4 in the bottom of the eighth thanks to a Remy double and then singles by Yastrzemski, Carlton Fisk, and Lynn.

In the ninth, a one-out walk to Burleson gave Red Sox fans hope, and Remy lined a hit to right that had trouble written all over it. Yankees right fielder Piniella lost sight of it but went "to where I thought it would land," and stabbed it just before it skipped past him. Burleson, thinking Piniella had a chance to catch the ball in the air, stopped at second, then moved to third on a Rice fly out. Yaz stepped up with a chance to at least tie the game, but popped up a 1-0 pitch that Yankees third baseman Graig Nettles squeezed in foul territory behind third to give New York the AL East crown.

Torrez, the last man to touch Dent's home run ball before it fell into the net, remains surprisingly affable about the whole deal. This always has infuriated a faction of the Boston fandom. Torrez remains a happy-go-lucky soul, the same guy who was heard screaming, "I'm off the hook!" as he prowled the bowels of Shea Stadium in the minutes after Bill Buckner's Game 6 gaffe.

"I pitched a great game," Torrez reminds us. "You can give me credit or not, but it was a great game to pitch. To hold that club to zero runs with two outs in the seventh. Hey, in today's game, they'd have already called in somebody else for relief. Bob Stanley came in and gave up the RBI double to Munson and the home run to Jackson. How come he never gets blamed?"

How much of a sport is Torrez about this whole thing? In 1989, he flew to Delray Beach, Fla., and participated in a publicity stunt to christen Dent's baseball academy. Dent built a mini-Fenway and opened the ballpark by hitting another homer off a smiling, gopher-ball-throwing Torrez. The re-enactment was a hit. Dent hit Torrez's fifth pitch over the Wall of Little Fenway. It was enough to make any Sox fan reach for a barf bag.

"We sign autographs together," says Torrez. "It's kept my name in the paper. Other than the Shot Heard 'Round the World, it's probably the most famous home run ever. I pitched my butt off in that game and I have nothing to be ashamed of."

Yastrzemski, who was the man closest to the ball when it sailed over the wall, says, "I didn't think it was going into the net. I thought it would hit the wall, but it kept carrying. When it went into the net, I had a sinking feeling. They were lucky like that all day. Piniella made that play when he lost the ball in the sun. The Curse. Everything went in their favor."

When Dent hit it, he didn't think his fly ball was going over the wall. He ran hard, rounded first, and saw the umpire's signal. Home run. Dent never saw the ball sail into the net. It was his fifth homer of the season. He hit 40 in his career.

Many years later, he sat in the Monster Seats for a game.

"It was a lot of fun," he says. "Guys were telling me they remembered when they were 12 years old and I broke their hearts and ruined their lives. They're just good baseball fans up there."

And the "B.F. Dent" handle? "That's what they always put above my locker in the visitor's room at Fenway when I came back there."

Ken Fratus, Globe Staff, contributed to this report. ❖

Right: Dent felt the love when he put his team ahead.

MORE HEARTBREAK IN THE BRONX

And so a new generation of New Englanders, circa 2003, learned the risk of rooting for the Red Sox.

Just as so many of their predecessors had done, the 2003 edition teased their fans for months. They said they were different from their forebears. They claimed that what happened before had nothing to do with them. They made everyone believe this really was the year.

Right: The dugout wasn't a happy place for Pedro Martinez, who got no help from above in this night's losing effort.
Below: Grady Little left Martinez in the game, then watched as it all unraveled.

WHO	**RED SOX** VS. **YANKEES.**
WHERE	**YANKEE STADIUM,** NEW YORK.
WHEN	**OCTOBER 16, 2003.**
WHY THE DRAMA	Same curse, different year. Bucky (Bleeping) Dent, meet Aaron (Bleeping) Boone.

But in the end, they fell — in excruciating fashion. The weight of the Boston uniform is always too heavy.

Meet the new Red Sox. Same as the old Red Sox. In perhaps the most painful game in franchise history — no small statement given the Sox' penchant for macabre moments — the Sox lost the American League pennant to their century-old nemesis, the New York Yankees.

Aaron Boone's 11th-inning, first-pitch, walkoff homer off Tim Wakefield at 12:16 in the morning gave the Yankees a 6-5, Game 7 victory over the Sox, putting New York in the World Series against Florida. Naturally, Boone is the grandson of Ray Boone, a longtime Red Sox scout.

Cover your eyes, Sox fans — it gets worse. Boston led, 4-0 in the fifth and 5-2 in the eighth. Like their Cub cousins earlier in this postseason, the Sox were five outs away with a three-run lead. Champagne was chilling.

But before you could say Calvin Schiraldi, Pedro Martinez coughed up four straight hits, three runs, and the American League pennant. Maybe this was revenge for the night Pedro said, "Wake up the Bambino. Bring him back and I'll drill him."

Fittingly, Martinez was KO'd by a bloop two-run double to center by Jorge Posada. That's the same Posada who engaged in an angry exchange with Martinez during Game 3 after Pedro hit Karim Garcia.

It didn't take days, weeks, or months to find the Game 7 goat. Say hello to Sox manager Grady Little, who joins Dennny Galehouse, Johnny Pesky, Bill Buckner, Mike Torrez, John McNamara, the aforementioned Schiraldi, and Bob Stanley in the Sox collection of dartboard ornaments.

Little left Martinez in the game long after it was clear the fragile ace was done. It was surprising to see Pedro start the eighth let alone surrender a long, one-out double to Derek Jeter.

After another base hit, Grady went to the mound. Relievers were ready. Nothing. Hideki Matsui cracked a hard double to right. Still no hook from the manager. Martinez was left to face Posada, who more than evened the score in their personal war with the bloop double to center. That tied the game and finally Little came out to get Martinez.

The manager said Martinez told him he wanted to stay in the game when he went out for the first visit.

After the fateful Yankee eighth, there was an air of cursed inevitability surrounding the proceedings. The Sox weren't able to do anything with Yankee closer Mariano Rivera and it was just a matter of time before someone broke through against a weary Wakefield. ❖

GAME 1 / OCTOBER 8	R	H	E
RED SOX	5	13	0
YANKEES	2	3	0

GAME 2 / OCTOBER 9	R	H	E
RED SOX	2	10	1
YANKEES	6	8	0

GAME 3 / OCTOBER 11	R	H	E
YANKEES	4	7	0
RED SOX	3	6	0

GAME 4 / OCTOBER 13	R	H	E
YANKEES	2	6	1
RED SOX	3	6	0

GAME 5 / OCTOBER 14	R	H	E
YANKEES	4	7	1
RED SOX	2	6	1

GAME 6 / OCTOBER 15	R	H	E
RED SOX	9	16	1
YANKEES	6	12	2

GAME 7 / OCTOBER 16	R	H	E
RED SOX	5	11	0
YANKEES	6	11	1

Grady Little's decision not to pull Pedro Martinez in the eighth was bewildering. Martinez had documented trouble beyond the seventh inning in 2003 and, to make matters worse, there were two well-rested relievers ready in the bullpen. One of those relievers, Mike Timlin, had not allowed a single hit in this ALCS.

TED WILLIAMS WALKS OFF WITH ALL-STAR WIN

Teddy Ballgame might as well have been Teddy All-Star Game. Not only did he enjoy the greatest individual performance in the game's history, bashing two homers in a 12-0 American League victory in 1946, but Williams hit the most dramatic home run in All-Star history — a three-run, game-winning blast in the ninth at Briggs Stadium (later Tiger Stadium) in the mythic summer of 1941.

Williams was en route to his .406 season and Joe DiMaggio was in the midst of his 56-game hitting streak when the All-Star Game came to Detroit. At the break, DiMaggio's streak was at 48 games and Williams was batting .405.

Williams drove in the American League's first run with a fourth-inning double, but the AL trailed, 5-3, and Williams was due up sixth in the bottom of the ninth.

Ken Keltner reached on a one-out infield single to start the rally, then Joe Gordon singled and Cecil Travis walked. Joltin' Joe was next, and he hit what should have been a game-ending double play, but a sliding Travis disrupted Billy Herman at second and forced a bad throw. Keltner scored and that brought Williams to the plate with two on, two out, and the AL trailing, 5-4.

Cub righty Claude Passeau, who had fanned Williams in the eighth, was on the mound. The 22-year-old hitter fouled the first pitch, then took two balls. He turned on the next offering, launching a game-winning, three-run bomb into the stands in right, clapping his hands and jumping for joy as he rounded the bases.

Dominic DiMaggio, Williams's teammate and Joe's brother, had a great view as Williams dug in. "They had a powwow on the mound and I was in the on-deck circle, thinking they'd walk Ted to get to me. But they pitched to Ted and, oh God, it was only a matter of if that ball was going to stay in the park. Ted was prancing up and down. I can't ever remember seeing him so happy."

Later, Williams tried to downplay the event as merely "one of my highlights," but in his autobiography he referred to the home run as "the most thrilling hit of my life."

Above: The splendid skills of Ted Williams made him a threat every time he stepped onto the field.
Right: Though he refused to tip his hat on the field, even Teddy Ballgame knew that a guy couldn't be a star without occasionally acknowledging his fans in the stands.

Baseball

WHO	**AMERICAN LEAGUE** VS. **NATIONAL LEAGUE.**
WHERE	**BRIGGS STADIUM,** DETROIT.
WHEN	**JULY 8, 1941.**
WHY THE DRAMA	In a grandiose battle of baseball's biggest icons, legends, and stars, Teddy Ballgame shined the brightest.

	R	H	E
NATIONAL LEAGUE	5	10	2
AMERICAN LEAGUE	7	11	3

The last walkoff?

It should have come as no surprise to the Fenway fans when Ted Williams homered in his last at-bat on Sept. 28, 1960. You see, he had actually accomplished the feat six years earlier – sort of.

In the spring of 1954, writing an article for the Saturday Evening Post, Williams declared, "This is my last year." And though few believed him, Williams insisted he was serious.

On Sept.26, playing in Fenway against Washington in what appeared to be his last game, Williams strode to the plate leading off the seventh, the Red Sox up, 4-2. Suddenly realizing that this may be it, the fans gave The Kid a huge ovation. On the first pitch from Gus Keriazakos, Williams sent a drive into the right field stands for homer No.366.

As pointed out by Dick Johnson and Glenn Stout in their book,"Ted Williams: A Portrait in Words and Pictures," that very well could have been Williams's final at-bat. But Washington's pitching staff gave up four more runs in the inning, allowing Williams to bat once again, in the eighth, when he popped out.

As for his threat to retire, Williams stayed true to his word through spring training and the start of the '55 season. But on May 13, he reconsidered and signed a new contract, playing in his first game May 28. He would go on to bat .356 that season with 28 homers and 83 RBIs in 98 games. And he'd stick around for five more years.

APRIL 19, 1991 » BY NICK CAFARDO, GLOBE STAFF

BASEBALL'S LONGEST GAME

	1	2	3	4	5	6	7	8	9	10	11	12	13	14	15	16	17	18	19	20	21	22	23	24	25	26	27	28	29	30	31	32	33	R	H	E
RED WINGS	0	0	0	0	0	0	1	0	0	0	0	0	0	0	0	0	0	0	0	0	1	0	0	0	0	0	0	0	0	0	0	0	0	2	18	3
PAW SOX	0	0	0	0	0	0	0	0	1	0	0	0	0	0	0	0	0	0	0	0	1	0	0	0	0	0	0	0	0	0	0	0	1	3	21	1

Above: The scoreboard tells the story. It took 33 innings to end this game between Pawtucket and Rochester. On the upside: If you stuck around for all of it, you went home with a season's ticket.

Some great finishes happen in an instant — a fateful swing of a bat or swish of a net. Others go on all night.

In April of 1981 at Rhode Island's McCoy Stadium, the Pawtucket Red Sox played the first 32 innings off the longest game in professional baseball history. And even that wasn't enough to decide the matter.

The contest with the Rochester Red Wings that was finally suspended shortly after 4 in the morning resumed nine weeks and three days later (the next time the visitors came through Rhode Island). But by then the magic had dissipated. The PawSox prevailed 3-2 in the bottom off the 33rd.

The game was a memorable chapter in more than a half-dozen careers that would end up in the majors, including a few (Wade Boggs and Cal Ripken) that were destined for Cooperstown. It was an even bigger deal for the lesser known participants. For Dave Koza — who lined a sharp single to drive in Marty Barrett with the winning run — this was his finest moment.

"Other than getting married, this was the greatest thrill of my life," Koza later said of the hit that ended the eight-hour, 25-minute game.

Overall, PawSox pitchers combined for 34 strikeouts and 18 walks. Russ Laribee, who batted third for the PawSox, went 0 for 11 with seven strikeouts. Barrett went 2 for 12, Boggs 4 for 13.

"It was a cold, vicious night," recalled team president Mike Tamburro. "I left the park with the sun rising over the right-field fence. I went home to change and shower, went to the early Easter Mass and drove back here for an afternoon game at 1 p.m."

Tamburro said 19 fans (of the original total of 1,740) who watched the game from start to finish were rewarded with season tickets. Many others came and went, including nightshift factory workers and hospital staff.

"There was a doctor who had just delivered a baby who asked me what I was doing looking through that slot [in the wall in the back of the dugout]," recalled manager Joe Morgan, who had been ejected in the 22nd inning. "I said, 'I'm watching the game.' He didn't believe me. So we shared that small opening for a while."

As it turned out, the umpires' rule book was missing the section about an inning not starting after 12:50 a.m. Not long after 2 a.m., the omission was noted but the game went on. A call went out to International League president Harold Cooper at around 3. Cooper called back shortly after 4 and suggested it was time to suspend it.

The classic story from the game involved Pawtucket right-hander Luis Aponte, who pitched four scoreless innings (the seventh through the 11th) and got a ride home from teammate Mike Smithson at around 3:30 a.m. When Aponte got to his Pawtucket apartment, his wife refused to let him in.

"He came back to the car and he asks me to take him back to the ballpark," Smithson told the Pawtucket Times. "He said, 'My wife won't let me in. She thought I was out drinking all night.' " ❖

Baseball

REGULAR SEASON GAME

WHO	**PAWTUCKET RED SOX** VS. **ROCHESTER RED WINGS.**
WHERE	**MCCOY STADIUM,** PAWTUCKET, RHODE ISLAND.
WHEN	**APRIL 18, 1981.**
WHY THE DRAMA	Some minor league games just feel endless. This one practically was.

	R	H	E
ROCHESTER RED WINGS	2	18	3
PAWTUCKET RED SOX	3	21	1

Bat fuel

Just how cold was it during The Longest Game? According to one report, the thermometer hit 28 degrees — cold enough that players burned bats to keep warm.

"I think we started out that fire with charcoal and then threw in some bats," confirms PawSox trainer Dale Robertson. "Anything that was flammable at that point. If you weren't moving around, you were going to stiffen up. Everyone was trying to stay motivated, saying, 'Get up, go get 'em.' "

Even though most of the fans got up and got out, the game may have been a franchise-saver.

"The good Lord loved us," PawSox owner Ben Mondor said, chortling at the memory. "He not only blessed us with an event that happened once in 140 years, but the major leagues went on strike."

All the media outlets that normally would have been preoccupied with the big boys sent reporters and camera crews to Pawtucket. Not only was The New York Times there, but the BBC, Armed Forces Radio, and TV stations from Tokyo. Umpires granted special dispensation to the photographers lined up along both baselines.

"Suddenly," team president Mike Tamburro said, "people in Rhode Island and southern New England realized something important could happen at this little ballpark on Columbus Avenue."

ANOTHER SUPER-CLOSE SUPER BOWL

SUPER BOWL XXXVIII

After their second wonderfully dramatic Super Bowl triumph, it was officially OK to place the New England Patriots in a rarely deserved, historical sentence. A fan could call them one of the greatest teams of all time and could do so without apologizing or blinking or giving a monologue on this era of free agency.

When a team wins a second championship in three years it is officially great. Swallow it straight with no chaser.

A few things were established when the Patriots won Super Bowl XXXVIII, 32-29, over the Carolina Panthers:

■ Adam Vinatieri officially became one of the best clutch athletes New England sports fans have ever seen. We're not just talking about clutch kickers or clutch football players. We're talking athletes, regardless of the sport and regardless of the decade. After Carolina's huge comeback, Vinatieri and his teammates could also start their own drama club.

■ After his second winning, 90-second Super Bowl drive, Tom Brady had to make room for another MVP Cadillac in his garage.

■ Bill Belichick solidified his status as the top head coach in the NFL, Scott Pioli stood tall as the league's leading personnel man, and Robert Kraft settled in as the most exceptional of Paul Tagliabue's 32 owners.

This Patriots team was brilliantly built, in such a way that one man could not disrupt the system. It was built with corny words — "spirit" and "soul" and "integrity."

"Here's all you have to know about our team," Belichick said. "We won all those games in a row, and not one person wants to take credit for it. Not one guy. Brady credits the offensive line. The coaches credit the players. Ty (Law) got three interceptions in the AFC Championship game, and he says the pressure from the defensive line made it possible.

"How cool is that?"

Probably as cool as Brady in the fourth quarter of this game. The Patriots were leading, 21-16, and were one score from putting the Panthers in a difficult position. On third down at the Carolina 9, Brady threw a pass intended for Christian Fauria. It was intercepted. Carolina turned the turnover into a touchdown that put the Panthers ahead, 22-21.

Then Brady came back with a touchdown to Mike Vrabel — Mike Vrabel! — and watched Kevin Faulk complete the 2-point conversion. Carolina responded with a touchdown, and then Brady again put Vinatieri in position to make a game-winning, 41-yard kick.

No, they weren't scary, not like the Steel Curtain Steelers of the mid to late 1970s or the undefeated Dolphins of '72. Belichick didn't stalk the sideline like a Vince Lombardi or Bill Parcells.

Left and right: Adam Vinatieri kicked the game-winning field goal in Super Bowl XXXVIII, just as he had in 2002.

WHO	**PATRIOTS** VS. **PANTHERS.**
WHERE	**RELIANT STADIUM,** HOUSTON.
WHEN	**FEBRUARY 1, 2004.**
WHY THE DRAMA	Deja vu all over again. A gutsy, Tom Brady-led final drive culminates in Adam Vinatieri's game-winning 41-yard field goal with four seconds left.

On a roll

This never gets old: Tom Brady marching his grizzled infantry downfield in the final minutes, Adam Vinatieri booting the pigskin between the uprights as if on cue, jubilation running through the streets of New England. Again.

After the Pats captured their second Lombardi trophy in 2004, the question went from "how on earth?" to "how many can these guys win?" Then Bill Belichick's men kept the dynasty talk rolling with an emphatic Super Bowl victory in 2005, their third title in four years. Though the drama was toned down, the Pats prevailed by the same 3-point margin, this time 24-21 over the Philadelphia Eagles.

How many more times can they pull off a super close win in a super-sized game? Who knows. But we wouldn't bet against them.

Above: Second verse, same as the first? Jubilant Patriots stormed the field in Houston, announcing to the world that this close victory meant just as much as it had two years prior in New Orleans.
Left: Vinatieri knew to brace for the inevitable gang tackle by teammates after his championship-caliber boot.

A season of drama

◈ Every team destined for a season of greatness has at least one improbable victory. For the Patriots, it came Oct. 19 in South Florida. Playing without four defensive stalwarts and with the history of an 0-13 record in Miami in September and October, New England prevailed, 19-13, in overtime on an 82-yard touchdown pass from Tom Brady to Troy Brown — the Patriots' longest pass play of the season.

◈ New England sports fans who lost sleep during the baseball playoffs returned to their late-night ways in early November of 2003, tuning in to "Monday Night Football" to watch the Patriots play at Denver. But this time, there was a reward for staying up late. In a game it appeared they had no chance to win, the Patriots beat the Broncos, 30-26, on the strength of genius moves by Belichick (including an intentional safety) and another big-time performance from Brady (20 of 35, 350 yards). The winning TD came with 30 seconds left when Brady connected with David Givens on an 18-yard touchdown pass.

◈ In the 2004 conference semifinal clash with Tennessee, the Patriots made it a lucky 13 in a row with a bone-chilling 17-14 playoff win over the Titans on the frozen tundra of New England's Gillette Stadium. In a time-tested formula, mildly reminiscent of the Snow Bowl playoff win over Oakland two years before, Adam Vinatieri's 46-yard field goal with 4:06 remaining broke a late tie.

But the 2003-'04 Patriots were resourceful. They could win games with defense or by topping 30 points. They could win in nasty conditions (the AFC East clincher over Miami). They could win ugly games (9-3 over Cleveland, 17-6 over the New York Giants), and games that just may be considered the most thrilling in league history.

The Patriots' victory over the Rams in Super Bowl XXXVI was like that. So was their win two years later.

The Panthers? It must be said that the losing team was outstanding in this game. New England, though, was just a little better and a little tougher. And that's the way the Patriots played all season. They were fallible enough to make every opponent believe it had a chance, but skilled and creative enough to handle every tough situation. ❖

THE DAY THE MVP WAS A TRACTOR

The play came right out of the Heavy Equipment Catalog, went by the name of John Deere 314, and was the best sweep ever run by the 1982-'83 Patriots. And the guy who ran the sweep that beat the despised Dolphins was on leave for the day from the Norfolk state prison — it's the truth, the whole truth, and nothing but the truth, so help me, Pete Rozelle.

Below: New England players make way for Mark Henderson's moment of fame aboard the tractor that cleared the way for John Smith's game-winning field goal.

Above: In one of the most bizarre games ever played in the NFL, New England and Miami struggled just to keep their footing on the snowy, icy field at Schaefer Stadium. If only they'd known earlier that winterized heavy equipment was allowed.

For eons and eons, the Patriots searched for the big play in tight moments to win the close games. Players, coaches, quarterbacks, placekickers, and fortunetellers came and went, promising all but delivering the accustomed painful loss. But Mark Henderson, an inmate serving 15 years for burglary, stole one from Don Shula and the Dolphins on December 12.

First, last and foremost, New England beat Miami, 3-0, on the skating rink at snowbound Schaefer Stadium when John Smith kicked a 33-yard field goal with less than five minutes left in the game. That's just the bare facts, ma'am; there's much more to this tale.

With both teams skidding and soft-stepping to what seemed an inevitable 0-0 overtime tie, the Patriots stalled at the Miami 16-yard line with 4:45 to go. The Dolphins weren't overly concerned. The teams had Laurel-and-Hardied through two earlier field-goal misses, and history had never recorded a field goal being kicked during a hockey game.

The idea to clear a spot for Smith to try a 33-yard field goal was jokingly suggested by quarterback Steve Grogan. Coach Ron Meyer then ran down the sideline frantically waving at Henderson and his tractor as Smith scuffed his foot into the frozen turf to try to break up the ice.

Henderson set out immediately along the 20-yard line "and we didn't think anything of it, "said Miami's Bob Baumhower. "He'd been driving the thing around all day clearing the lines."

But then the John Deere took a sharp left turn to where Smith and teammate Matt Cavanaugh were chipping away, seven yards behind the line of scrimmage. The tractor's rotating broom began sweeping away all the snow in front of it. Presto! Smith now had a pristine patch of turf from which to kick."

"When we saw what was happening from the sidelines, we cheered," said the Patriots' Mosi Tatupu. "We were laughing. We couldn't believe it."

The Dolphins, meanwhile, were dumbfounded. "One moment the guy is right there in front of us and then he made a turn and went over there seven yards behind the line of scrimmage," said Baumhower. "I'd say it was a little unusual; it shouldn't have happened."

For the record, Smith's snow-plow-assisted field goal was his first game-winning three-pointer with the Patriots. ❖

Ron Borges, Globe Staff, contributed to this report.

Football

REGULAR SEASON GAME

WHO	PATRIOTS VS. DOLPHINS.
WHERE	SCHAEFER STADIUM, FOXBOROUGH, MASSACHUSETTS.
WHEN	DECEMBER 12, 1982.
WHY THE DRAMA	What do you get when you combine an icy field, a tractor, and a prison inmate? A play the Dolphins can't defend.

John Smith, kicker

Before Adam Vinatieri's playoff wizardry put the "ooh" and "ahhh" in Patriots football, there was another field goal kicker making noise in New England. A native of Southampton, England, John Smith was fighting off pro soccer recruiters as a teenager before his reputation landed him a tryout with the Pats and a position with the team in 1974. He had never heard of the National Football League. He had never heard of football played with hands and helmets. Heck, he played in the first American game he ever saw.

He set several impressive franchise marks during his 10-year career, including making all 51 of his point-after-touchdown attempts in 1980, a club record. That success led to a spot on the 1981 AFC Pro Bowl team. In short, he was as consistent as the US Postal Service.

"But all anyone remembers is the darn snow kick," Smith carped to the Globe's Scott Thurston in 1989. "That's my claim to fame."

Actually, former teammates also remember Smith's tireless work ethic — riding his bike back and forth to the stadium every day in the offseason, shoveling off the field so he could work at his craft. His approach to the game became his real legacy.

"Nothing just appears in life, does it? You have to work at it and develop it," Smith explained. "There's always someone coming around the corner who's better than you are."

JANUARY 20, 2002 ❱❱ BY BOB RYAN, GLOBE STAFF

ROUGHING THE PASSER?
GIVE US A BREAK

WARNING: The following tale may not be suitable for all ages. If you're the type who's taught your offspring that life is fair, that good deeds are rewarded, that there is always justice for all — of course if you really believe this, you may already be beyond parenting help — and that athletic contests cannot be controlled by officials, then don't let your kids read any further.

For this is a saga of aggravation, frustration, and infuriating injustice. Life is most certainly not always fair and the best team does not always win. On Dec. 18, 1976, the New England Patriots had a playoff game stolen from them by the Oakland Raiders, 24-21 (capped off by a late Kenny Stabler touchdown run), and by an officiating crew for whom there should be reserved a special place in athletic Hades.

The first three quarters were a Patriots fan's dream. First, Russ Francis put the Patriots ahead, 14-10, on a 26-yard TD reception from Steve Grogan. Then Jess Phillips capped a drive with the 3-yard run needed to make it 21-10 midway through the third.

Good Lord, I thought, the Patriots are going to the Super Bowl. Until that day, I just didn't know how good they were. Sure, Grogan had run for an amazing 12 touchdowns that year, and I knew about John Hannah, Sam Cunningham, Mike Haynes, Francis, etc., and that they had gone 11-3. But they were a 3-11 team the year before, and they were still the Patriots.

Now I'm going to cut to the chase: Most fans have read and heard about the roughing-the-passer flag that referee Ben Dreith threw on Ray "Sugar Bear" Hamilton on a third-and-18 Stabler incompletion at the Patriots' 27 with 57 seconds left and the Patriots leading, 21-17. Though the call was wrong and inappropriate (you don't make a borderline call in such a situation — this was absolutely borderline), it wasn't the worst call of the day.

The worst officiating travesty came earlier in the fourth. The Patriots were driving and had third and 5 at the Oakland 32. The play call was a pass to Francis, the noted tight end, and it was incomplete — for a very good reason. Linebacker Phil Villapiano had attached himself to Francis right from the snap. Neither Dreith nor any of his colleagues saw fit to call the most obvious interference call any of them would ever encounter, period.

It wasn't just these two calls/non-calls, either. It was the brutal incompetence of the officiating all afternoon. How could Stabler go back to pass 49 times without there once being a holding call on his line, a line that was well known as the holdingest bunch in captivity?

The Patriots wuz robbed. And worse yet, the damnable Al Davis Raiders who benefited from this injustice went on to win that Super Bowl. But I just know that in their deepest heart of hearts the most rational among them know it was tainted, and that in a fair world they would have been eliminated in the first round. ❖

Right: A favorite go-to guy for Steve Grogan's passing attack, tight-end Russ Francis helped put the Pats ahead, but then couldn't persuade the refs to call an obvious interference penalty against Oakland in the fourth quarter.

AFC DIVISIONAL PLAYOFF

WHO	**PATRIOTS** VS. **RAIDERS.**
WHERE	**OAKLAND COLISEUM,** OAKLAND.
WHEN	**DECEMBER 18, 1976.**
WHY THE DRAMA	The Pats thought they had this game won until a controversial call turned the tables. Payback was served in 2002.

The pain game

The 1976 Pats had the momentum, they had the coaching, and they had the talent. In fact, they almost had it all.

What has made the infamous roughing-the-passer call so difficult for Pats fans to swallow is that many consider the 1976 team among the most talented in franchise history. With guys like Steve Grogan, John Hannah, and Ray Hamilton, it was a team that coulda, shoulda, woulda won the big one. But anyone who has followed Boston sports for more than a few years knows that the Red Sox have no monopoly on cursed endings. In fact, prior to the Tom Brady era, big-game losses seemed scripted for the Patriots.

Back in 1964, New England was upended 51-10 by San Diego in the AFL Championship. In Super Bowl XX, the good guys' 3-0 lead turned into a brutal 46-10 pounding at the hands of Mike Ditka's Chicago Bears. In 1997, Bret Favre's Green Bay Packers bested the boys from Foxborough 35-21 in Super Bowl XXXI, which included a 99-yard kickoff return for a game-clinching touchdown. Crushing.

But what both the Patriots and Red Sox have found in the 21st Century is that clutch plays, storybook endings, victory parades, and trophy tours can pardon a lot of bad memories. Yes, Al Davis's Oakland Raiders will always have 1976. But thanks to the 2002 "Snow Bowl" and a beautiful little thing known as the tuck rule, Bob Kraft's New England Patriots have a dynasty.

DREW BLEDSOE'S TELLTALE DISPLAY OF HEART

Seventy passes.

At the end of a wonderful, historic afternoon in the cheap-o, concrete slab known as Foxboro Stadium, what stood out most was the number 70. The 1994 New England Patriots, who appeared hopelessly beaten by the first-place Minnesota Vikings, came back from a 20-0 deficit late in the second quarter to take back the day, 26-20, in overtime. It went down as one of the most thrilling and spirited Patriots comebacks since Billy Sullivan was awarded the AFL's eighth and final franchise in 1959.

Right: The Vikings never adjusted to the Patriots' second-half game plan, which made for a clash that New England ultimately dominated.
Below: Not only did the Patriots quarterback take it to the air 70 times; he also wasn't shy about moving the ball forward himself, when necessary. Oh, and he threw zero interceptions. It was that kind of day.

Football

REGULAR SEASON GAME

WHO	**PATRIOTS** VS. **VIKINGS.**
WHERE	**FOXBORO STADIUM,** FOXBOROUGH, MASSACHUSETTS.
WHEN	**NOVEMBER 13, 1994.**
WHY THE DRAMA	Football doesn't get more fun than watching a quarterback complete 45 of 70 passes en route to a 26-20 overtime win.

It was a game that produced a lot of second-half memories and goofy numbers, but what was most memorable was the performance of New England's sophomore quarterback. Drew Bledsoe threw 70 passes, completing 45 for 426 yards. He threw three touchdown passes and had zero interceptions, as in 0 for 70.

Nobody had ever thrown 70 passes in an NFL game. Not Slingin' Sammy Baugh, Otto Graham, or Norm Van Brocklin. Not Y.A. Tittle, Johnny Unitas, or Bart Starr. Not Joe Namath, Joe Montana, or Dan Marino.

Fans knew as they exited the stadium that someday they'd be able to tell the kids they were there the day Drew let it fly 70 times. Of course, 45 completions was also an amazing number, and an NFL record. It was one of those rare Foxboro Stadium days when the throws actually outnumbered the throw-ups.

Bledsoe had taken some heat in the weeks leading up to this game. He hadn't thrown a touchdown pass in almost a month but had tossed 11 interceptions in New England's previous four games (all losses). He'd been booed when he came off the Foxboro Stadium field after an ugly game against Miami. There was plenty of talk (and ink) about him being beaten-down and battered, patting the ball, tipping off his passes.

So he went out and completed more passes in a game than anyone in the long history of the National Football League, winning the game with his final heave, a 14-yard TD strike to Kevin Turner.

After the game, Bledsoe also embraced the inevitable question about "answering his critics."

"In the past few weeks, I've had some bad games," Bledsoe said. "But I want everybody to realize I'm here for the long haul. I'm going to be the Patriots' quarterback for a while, barring injury. There'll be some bad games and some good games, but I'll be here. Personally, I'm not going to get too high after games like this, or too low after games when I throw four interceptions."

The kid was right out of Central Casting. He didn't brag or hang his head. And week after week, he carried the load for this undermanned team. His receivers had dropped dozens of balls, but he never complained.

After a scoreless first half, New England chucked its unworkable game plan and came out running its two-minute, no-huddle offense. The Vikings never adjusted and eventually went back to Minnesota wondering what hit them. In the final two quarters, Bledsoe was an unfathomable 37 of 53 for 354 yards. ❖

"I'm here for the long haul," Drew Bledsoe said in the glow of his shining moment. Tom Brady was still in high school at the time.

THE FIRST TIME BOSTON COLLEGE KICKED NOTRE DAME'S BUTT

Boston College 41, Notre Dame 39 is the biggest achievement in the history of BC football.

That's right. The 1993 victory is bigger than the 1940 Georgetown game, bigger than the 1941 Sugar Bowl, and bigger than anything the Flutie teams ever did, the Miracle in Miami included.

The magnitude of the victory is in direct proportion to the nature of the opponent. With all due respect to the many significant triumphs in the BC past, finally beating undefeated, No. 1-ranked Notre Dame in South Bend meant more to the Boston College community than all the others put together. There is, after all, only one Notre Dame.

There are many football traditions: Michigan, USC, Alabama. Starting in the early 1980s, Miami developed a tradition. Even Harvard has one.

Traditions abound, but only Notre Dame has a mystique. You can't imagine the full scope of it until you've been to the hallowed campus in north-central Indiana. Visitors gawk at the sights (Touchdown Jesus… the Grotto… Sacred Heart Basilica… the Golden Dome) and know their team is facing the challenge of its life.

Notre Dame has something everyone else wants, and no one has been more envious of the ND football program than the people at Boston College, who battled for many a year just to set up a regular series of games with the Fighting Irish.

By the time the 1993 matchup rolled around (the fifth ever between the schools, Notre Dame having dominated the first four contests), the dust had cleared and there were only two Catholic schools left playing big-time football. Notre Dame monopolized the attention and the booty attendant to football success, and BC wanted a piece of the action; it was that simple.

The BC football program never was going to completely validate itself until it beat Notre Dame.

On a special day in 1993, no person calling himself or herself a sports fan was unaware of the last-second, game-winning David Gordon 41-yard field goal by 11 o'clock in the evening. The entire sports world knew that quarterback Glenn Foley and Gordon and a planeload of Boston College players and coaches led by head man Tom Coughlin had gone into Notre Dame Stadium and beaten the top-ranked Fighting Irish, despite ND's nearly game-saving fourth-quarter comeback run of 22 unanswered points.

BC beating Notre Dame — and for the first time destroying ND's national championship hopes in the process — must be regarded as the biggest local college story ever. BC football is clearly the pre-eminent local college sports entity in Massachusetts, an unarguable premise despite the Boston University NCAA hockey titles, the many Harvard achievements, and the BC basketball Sweet 16 forays. And BC's 1993 football team didn't just beat Notre Dame, it took down one of the best Notre Dame teams of the past quarter century, in a dramatic game worthy of 10 highlight films.

Final score, again: Boston College 41, Notre Dame 39. ❖

College

FOOTBALL / REGULAR SEASON GAME

WHO	**BOSTON COLLEGE** VS. **NOTRE DAME.**
WHERE	**NOTRE DAME STADIUM,** SOUTH BEND, INDIANA.
WHEN	**NOVEMBER 20, 1993.**
WHY THE DRAMA	That guy Flutie and his teammates? They had a nice run, but they didn't notch the greatest victory in Boston college sports history. Here's who did.

They had it coming

Just scheduling enough games with Notre Dame to give Boston College a decent shot at competitiveness was a Herculean task.

The first BC-Notre Dame confrontation finally came about in 1975 — after many, many years of BC pleas — because then athletic director Bill Flynn probably had more personal friends than any man in college football. One of his closest amigos was former Notre Dame AD Ed (Moose) Krause. Moose had sufficient clout to convince the Notre Dame clerics that giving a game to Boston College would neither taint Notre Dame men in this life nor doom their progeny to eternal damnation.

So the series began in 1975 with a 17-3 Notre Dame victory in Foxborough, Massachusetts. The next meeting was the 1983 Liberty Bowl, followed by a game in South Bend four years later, and the infamous 54-7 humiliation in 1992. After four games, the series stood ND 4, BC 0, and given the scope of that last triumph it felt more like ND 44, BC 0.

But as it turned out, Boston College had finally faced the Irish enough times to know what it took to prevail. And they had clearly suffered enough embarrassment to ensure maximum motivation.

Left: A lot more than just a game was riding on Dave Gordon's kick.

HARVARD BEATS YALE, 29-29

The year was 1968, the date Nov. 23, the place Harvard Stadium, and the winner Yale — at least, that's the way it looked late in the fourth quarter with the Elis leading, 29-13.

Neither team could have predicted what was about to happen, but what did occur helped turn the Harvard-Yale rivalry into The Game.

In the gathering dusk of a magical late Saturday afternoon, backup quarterback Frank Champi engineered one of the most implausible comebacks in history, guiding underdog Harvard to 16 points in the final 42 seconds.

The official final score was 29-29, but the result was recorded as a Harvard triumph. And the 1968 teams, who both finished 8-0-1, became a huge part of the lore of The Game, and of college sports in general.

"I don't like to relive things," Everett, Massachusetts native Champi said later. "But I remember my roommate Mel Craig said he had a dream. He told me it was about what actually happened. The whole week had a special feeling to it… a strange feeling."

Yale was supposed to be the clearly superior undefeated team entering this Ivy League title showdown. The Elis had a mystical quarterback named Brian Dowling, who had never lost a game he had finished since the sixth grade, and a running back, Calvin Hill, who would later star in the NFL.

Sure enough, the visitors raced out to a 22-0 lead, prompting Harvard coach John Yovicsin to insert Champi into the lineup, replacing George Lalich. After a 15-yard touchdown pass to Bruce Freeman late in the first half and Gus Crim's third-quarter touchdown run, the Crimson was within 22-13. But Dowling's fourth-quarter bootleg restored his team's comfortable lead.

A fumble gave Harvard the ball at its own 14 with 3:34 left and the ensuing drive featured a heads-up dash by Fritz Reed. He picked up what was controversially ruled a lateral on third-and-18 and raced all the way to a first down at the Yale 15. Champi's touchdown pass to Freeman and Crim's conversion run cut the lead in half.

After a successful onside kick, a long Champi run and a face mask penalty, it was first down for Harvard on the Yale 20. Then several incomplete passes, a Crim run to the 6, and a Champi 2-yard loss left time for one final play.

After fading back to pass, Champi was initially trapped, but then escaped and found Vic Gatto in the left corner of the end zone with no time left on the clock. A conversion pass to Pete Varney finished off the game.

The Tie sent legions of people into ecstasy as they swarmed onto the field. The Harvard Crimson came out with an edition featuring the headline, "HARVARD BEATS YALE, 29-29," and most who were there agreed with that assessment.

"We never felt we were tied," said longtime Yale coach Carm Cozza. "We felt we lost the game."

But what a game it was. ❖

Right: Frank Champi's two-point conversion pass to Harvard teammate Pete Varney finished off one of the most thrilling tie games ever played.

College

WHO	**HARVARD** VS. **YALE.**
WHERE	**HARVARD STADIUM,** CAMBRIDGE, MASSACHUSETTS.
WHEN	**NOVEMBER 23, 1968.**
WHY THE DRAMA	Sixteen points in 42 seconds, resulting in two undefeated teams. One of the greatest college football games ever played in New England.

"What I remember most," Harvard fullback Gus Crim told the Globe in 1993, "is in the third quarter [with the Eli up 29-13], the Yale handkerchiefs came out. You couldn't believe somebody had that audacity."

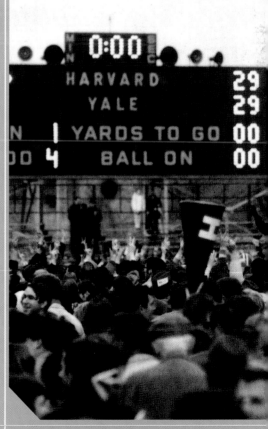

WHEN THE SUNS WENT DOWN IN TRIPLE OVERTIME

"People say to me," muses Curtis Perry, "'What's the best game you ever saw?' And I say, 'Well, there was this night in June, back in Boston ...'"

It was Friday, June 4, 1976, and it was Game 5 of the NBA Finals. Perry and his Phoenix Suns teammates were surprisingly alive, having tied the series at 2-2 with a pair of victories in Phoenix after being dismissed as pretenders following Boston's 98-87 and 105-90 dispatches in Games 1 and 2.

In this circumstance — 2-2 and coming back home — the Celtics felt invincible. In this particular case, they were also angry and determined to have vengeance. Their Game 3 loss had featured 65 fouls and 79 free throw attempts, which the Celtics believed represented officials kowtowing to the Suns' complaints about Boston's aggressiveness. Game 4 was no better, leading to a two-point Suns victory.

The Celtics weren't even supposed to be playing Phoenix, anyway. The NBA's anticipated apocalyptic confrontation that year was supposed to be defending champion Golden State, with the league's best record (59-23), against Boston, the champions once removed. But the 42-40 Phoenix squad upset Golden State in the Western Conference finals, winning Game 7 in Oakland when league MVP Rick Barry, apparently incensed because no teammate came to his aid when he engaged in first-period fisticuffs with brash Phoenix rookie Ricky Sobers, basically pouted for the remainder of the game. That prompted irreverent Phoenix scribe Joe Gilmartin to observe, "Old Chinese saying: 'Impossible to throw ball to man standing with arms folded.'"

When Game 5 began, the Celtics hit the ground defending, shooting, rebounding, passing, and, most of all, running. One reason was the return to the starting lineup of John Havlicek, who had been hobbling with a torn plantar fascia in his left foot.

Boston led by as many as 20 in the first half and by 16 in the third quarter and while Phoenix kept coming back, the Celtics were still in front by five heading into the fourth.

When Havlicek stuck one from the right baseline to make it 92-83, the fans thought it was over. But star guard Paul Westphal was about to assert himself, scoring 9 of his team's next 11 points including a three-point play with 39 seconds left that tied the score at 94.

With the score tied at 95 (Perry and Havlicek free throws), Dave Cowens deflected a Suns inbounds pass and Paul Silas tried to call for a timeout, unaware the Celtics had none left. Referee Richie Powers would not acknowledge the request. If he had, the Suns would have been shooting a potential game-winning technical foul.

It was a non-call that was still stuck in the Suns' craw months, years, even decades later.

"About two weeks later, a local Phoenix golf pro named Joe Porter was playing in the Westchester Classic," reports Jerry Colangelo, then the general manager and later the team's CEO. "He saw Richie Powers at the bar and he asked him why he didn't call that timeout. He said that Richie said, 'I didn't want Boston to lose like that.' If you ask me do I think he meant 'I didn't want Boston to lose like that,' or '[I didn't want] anyone to lose like that,' I'll say the latter."

Coach John MacLeod was not nearly so charitable. "What do I think he

Basketball

WHO	**CELTICS** VS **SUNS.**
WHERE	**BOSTON GARDEN.**
WHEN	**JUNE 4, 1976.**
WHY THE DRAMA	The Celts led by as many as 20 points. So how did this game go to triple overtime? Comebacks and controversy, of course.

Jo Jo never missed

The Celtics' victory over the fiery Phoenix Suns marked the Green Machine's 13th world championship and its second in three years. As is the case for every great Celtics team, the '76 version was led by veteran players, tireless coaches, and opportune role players. Jo Jo White, the C's aggressive point guard and series MVP, led all scorers with 33 points in the epic Game 5, and logged a vigorous 60 minutes of action on the parquet that night. Exceptional? Yes. Surprising? Not really.

Jo Jo (born John Henry White) was in marathon shape and was known as one of the original iron men in the sport. In a league that now puts a premium on three-point bombs and mid-air madness, White accomplished something far more impressive: he didn't miss a game for five years. That's half a decade. From 1973 through 1977, White played all 82 regular season games on the grueling NBA calendar.

A former marine, he was a classic three-sport athlete, drafted not only by the Celtics but also by Major League Baseball's Cincinnati Reds and the National Football League's Dallas Cowboys. He might have excelled at any of those pursuits, but the Boston Garden faithful are very glad he chose hoops.

meant?" he inquires. "BOSTON! He didn't want Boston to lose. Westphal would have made the technical foul and we would have won, and we would have won Game 6. I'm still angry."

Boston twice led by 4 in that first OT, but the Suns came back behind baskets by Perry and Heard to tie it at 101 and send it into a second OT. With 19 seconds left in that period, Jo Jo White sank a gorgeous running hook to make it 109-106. Suns done? Nah. Dick Van Arsdale hit a corner jumper, Westphal stole the ball and Perry eventually made a put-back for a one-point Suns lead.

Then it was Havlicek's turn for heroics. He banked in what seemed certain to be the game-winner.

Timekeeper Tony Nota did his job by allowing the clock to run out, despite the rather obvious fact there was at least one second, maybe two, at the Suns' disposal. The Celtics fought their way through the crowd into the locker room.

They soon returned but what they missed was chaos out on the floor. For openers, a blue-clad fan was attempting to wrestle referee Powers to the floor. Perry pulled the man off. Meanwhile, hundreds of people needed to be removed in order to resume the game with 00:01 put back on the clock.

Out of timeouts, the Suns needed to go 94 feet to score in one second. A technical foul (the Suns intentionally calling a timeout they didn't have) gave the Celtics a free throw but moved the inbounds pass to midcourt.

From there, Perry found Gar Heard, who was known for his jumper's extremely high arc. He let a patented moon shot fly from the top of the circle. The ball rattled home and the game was tied again.

In the third overtime, with Havlicek out of gas, Cowens gone, and Scott gone, the Celtic offense had become White, who would score 15 of his game-high 33 in the OTs and the unlikely Glen McDonald, a reserve who scored four in a row for a six-point Celtic lead.

Again the Suns came back and trailed by only two when Westphal just missed a last-second steal. White then dribbled out the clock and when the buzzer sounded, hooked a pass into the onrushing mob to cap off what many have called the greatest game ever played.

Game 6 was a predictable dud. The only regular who played anywhere near his capability was Charlie Scott, who had fouled out in 25 minutes on Friday (his fifth disqualification in five Finals games), and who had fresh enough legs to perform well (25 points, 11 rebounds, 5 steals) in the game that began a scant 39 1/2 hours later in Phoenix (12:30, local time).

The Suns actually edged ahead for a possession in the fourth quarter, but a 17-6 Boston run settled matters. The final was 87-80, and Boston was champion for the 13th time. ❖

Above and above left: Emotions ran high the whole time that Boston played Phoenix, and Dave Cowens was never one to hold back.

BIRD STOLE THE BALL

The replay was shown again. And again. And again. The little clock always started with five seconds in the corner and with all of that confusion on the screen.

"OK, last time," Celtics team services director Wayne Lebeaux said in the heat of the Boston Celtics' locker room after the game.

Twenty feet, maybe 30 feet from the parquet floor where all of this had really happened a few minutes earlier, Larry Bird stepped in front of Isiah Thomas's soft pass again and turned to whip the ball to Dennis Johnson again, and Johnson spun the ball into the basket and the wipe-your-eyes magic trick happened again — Boston Celtics 108, Detroit Pistons 107. Flat-out unbelievable, again.

"OK, one more time," Lebeaux said, whipping the tape back to the beginning. Even people who watch basketball films for a living could not see enough of this.

"I could see the ball was going to [Bill] Laimbeer," Bird explained. "I was going to foul him. I thought that if I fouled him right away, there'd only be four seconds left, and even if he made the shots, we'd still have a chance to tie the game.

"The ball just hung up there. I seemed to take forever to get to Laimbeer. I kept going and I got my left hand on the ball. I was thinking about shooting, but the ball was going the other way. Then I turned and saw Dennis. It was a lucky play. That was all it was."

He had gone for the game-winner and had been blocked by the Pistons' Dennis Rodman on an attempted drive. That was how the Pistons had possession at that end of the court, the ball skittering off Celts guard Jerry Sichting. But how was Bird still awake, not muttering at himself at that point in the game?

"How?" Celts assistant coach Chris Ford repeated when asked. "Because he's Larry Bird. That's the only reason I can think of."

Ford said he was standing, yelling the word "foul!" as the play was made. He never thought of a steal, never dreamed of it. Pistons coach Chuck Daly said he was standing and yelling "timeout!" without a prayer of being heard in this noisy turnaround fifth game of the 1987 Eastern Conference finals.

The amazing aspects of the play did not stop. There was a resemblance, perhaps, to the John Havlicek steal — "April 15, 1965," one reporter yelled across the room to another — but this was arguably even more significant. The Celtics did not have to score when Havlicek stole the ball; they only had to stop the Philadelphia villains from scoring.

Here the Celtics not only had to score, but Johnson had to make a shot that was approximately 9.8 on the degree-of-difficulty scale.

"You look at all the parts of that play, each one is amazing," Ford said. "Look at where Larry is [near the foul line]; at how far he has to come to steal the ball. Then you look at the fact that he's almost falling out of bounds and can't get a good shot. Then he sees DJ. Then DJ makes the shot. That was a harrrrd shot."

The tape showed that Johnson was coming for the basket almost as soon as Bird was stealing the ball.

"One more time," Lebeaux said. "Aw-www, the hell with that. I'm going to run this thing the whole damn night."

Grown men stood in the warm little room and stared. Again and again. Bird stole the ball. Johnson spun it into the basket. An entire city seemed to hop about an inch and a half off its feet. Again and again.

Larry Bird stole the ball. ❖

Right: Dennis Johnson and Larry Bird pulled off a bit of their own magic to end Game 5 with a win, 108-107.

Basketball

WHO	**CELTICS** VS. **PISTONS.**
WHERE	**BOSTON GARDEN.**
WHEN	**MAY 26, 1987.**
WHY THE DRAMA	Something about a pass that didn't quite go Detroit's way...

What Happened Next

Laker Magic

The Celtics went on to finish off the Pistons in Game 7, but the well-rested Lakers were another story. Game 4 of that series yielded Magic Johnson's sweetest moment — a running, across-the-key baby hook shot that sealed a 107-106 victory and gave Los Angeles a commanding 3-1 series edge. The 4-2 end result gave the Lakers their fourth of five championships in the '80s.

FOUR OT'S AND 50 POINTS FROM COUSY

In an individual basketball exhibition practically defying description, Celtics' great Bob Cousy steered his Boston club to a four-overtime 111-105 victory over the rugged Syracuse Nationals before 11,058 frenzied fans at the Boston Garden.

The March 21, 1953 performance probably ranks as Cousy's greatest-ever, and it's definitely what sealed the series win (2-0), vaulting the Celtics into the NBA semifinals against the New York Knicks.

WHAT COOZ DID:

1. Scored 50 points on 10 baskets and 30 free throws for a Garden/arena record and season's individual scoring mark, after scoring only seven points in the first half.

2. Scored 30 free tries in 32 "pressure" attempts.

3. Tied the game at the end of regulation play, 77-all, and the third of his successive free tosses sent the game into its first five-minute extra session.

4. Scored six points in the first extra session, including the last free throw which matched a Nats conversion to bring about a second extra session.

5. Scored two of four points in the second overtime to help bring about a third extra session, which started 90-all.

6. Scored eight of the Celtics' nine points in the third extra session, including two vital baskets. Here Cousy reached the greatest heights when, with time running out, he tied the game 97-all on two free throws. After Syracuse went ahead, 99-97, with three seconds remaining, he dropped in a beautiful one-hand push shot from 25 feet out to send the game into its fourth extra period, 99 apiece, as the crowd went wild.

7. Scored nine of the 12 points in the final period, sparking the Celtics from a five point, 104-99 deficit with three and one-half minutes remaining. Fans leaving the building were stopped in their tracks.

Cousy sank 18 successive free tries and played the last two overtime periods despite the onus of five personal fouls. The great backcourt ace was so exhausted that on two occasions during this three-hour, 11-minute epic he all but blew the game for the Celtics with a bad shot and a weird pass, which lost possession in vital moments.

The marvelous machinations of Cousy overshadowed a near-riot instigated by fisticuffs between Bob Brannum and Dolph Schayes at the half-way mark of the second period. Both players were ejected by referees Arnie Heft and Charley Eckman, who turned in nearly perfect officiating under the heaviest pressure.

Trailing by the aforementioned five in the final overtime, Cousy sank a free throw and batted home a rebound of a missed pop shot. He then stole a shallow Syracuse pass and went in alone for a soft left-hand backward two-pointer to knot the count as the crowd screamed. The teams went back and fourth for another minute or so, but soon Cousy was clinching the victory with four more free throws.

The legendary Celtics impresario Red Auerbach said it best. "Cousy? Don't get me started. I could go on all night on what the kid did. He's only the greatest." ❖

Bob Cousy was at the center of Celtics greatness long before anyone spoke of a green dynasty.

Basketball

WHO	**CELTICS** VS. **NATIONALS.**
WHERE	**BOSTON GARDEN.**
WHEN	**MARCH 21, 1953.**
WHY THE DRAMA	No shot clock, so Bob Cousy is in complete control, sinking 30 of 32 from the line.

The green machine

Robert Joseph Cousy, without whom there would have been no Boston Celtics for Bill Russell to lead in the direction of the 11 championships secured during Russell's tenure, played his final game in green in the spring of 1963. He sprained an ankle during the contest, which also happened to be the final game of that year's NBA postseason, but he returned because his team was in trouble against a dangerous Lakers squad. With The Cooz's firm hand on the tiller, the Celtics nailed down title No. 6 in the Los Angeles Sports Arena.

Cousy played seven years with Russell and one with John Havlicek, the championship playmaker who once told the Globe's Bob Ryan that as a rookie, "all I did was run around and make layups on passes from Cousy."

So many great players have performed for the Celtics that it's understandable if the names and achievements all sort of run together after awhile. It's hard now to conjure up the circumstance of the early '50s, when the Celtics had no cachet in Boston and the only reason most people went to see the team play was the electrifying and magnetic presence of the game's best passer, ballhandler, and thinker.

Absent Cousy, the Celtics would have quite literally ceased to exist.

HEINSOHN HEROICS AND THE START OF A BANNER RUN

WHO	**CELTICS** VS. **HAWKS.**
WHERE	**BOSTON GARDEN.**
WHEN	**APRIL 13, 1957.**
WHY THE DRAMA	Two overtimes. Two superstar frosh. One step closer to a dynasty.

The blood pressure of 13,909 rooters was pushed to the bursting point before the 1957 edition of the Boston Celtics finally edged the St. Louis Hawks, 125-123, in a double overtime thriller at the Garden to win their first National Basketball Association championship.

Although it was a team victory, owner Walter Brown had the firmest handshakes for Tommy Heinsohn, Frank Ramsey, Bill Russell, and a grand old pro, Arnie Risen.

Heinsohn, banishing any doubt that he was the freshman of the year, accounted for 37 points, 23 rebounds, and eight of the Celtics' 22 markers in the double overtime.

Russell scored the game-saving basket at the end of regulation play. Then he topped it with a tremendous block on Jack Coleman's shot which would have given the Hawks the victory.

In addition, the Celtics' second great freshman took 32 balls off the boards in a terrific defensive exhibition and counted three points in overtime.

Oddly, the Celts won with the greatest backcourt in pro ball's history — Bill Sharman and Bob Cousy — contributing only five floor baskets.

Cousy came through with 11 assists, but Sharman, appearing very "tight," did not have his soft shooting touch. Sharman hit only three in 20 from the floor; Cousy sank two of 20.

St. Louis fought hard all the way. Bob Pettit had 39 points, plus 19 rebounds and 11 of 13 at the line.

With the score in the second overtime tied at 121, Ramsey calmly converted a free try, then a 20-foot right-hand push shot from the outside key for a 124-121 lead as the house resounded with cheers.

But the Hawks weren't done. First Slater Martin sank a free throw cutting the Celts' lead to two, then he made a critical steal. After another free throw made it 124-123, the Hawks had a chance to pull ahead with one basket.

But with 17 seconds left, Alex Hannum was called for traveling.

After the Celtics brought the ball in, a desperate Hannum was all over Jim Loscutoff for a personal foul. Loscutoff made one then missed. After not one but two missed last-second shots, the Celtics finally were champs and Heinsohn was the hero. ❖

Left: Young guns Tom Heinsohn and Bill Russell delivered the Celtics' very first championship in a Game 7 battle that stretched into double overtime.

Totally Tommy

Tom Heinsohn left Union City, N.J., for Worcester, Massachusetts in the fall of 1952 and quickly became one of the best players in Holy Cross history. The 6-foot-7-inch forward, a consensus All-American his senior year, was the sophomore force behind the Crusaders' 1954 National Invitation Tournament championship team.

Red Auerbach snatched up Heinsohn in 1956, and the flat-topped forward with the stitched-up knee wrap immediately impressed with his shooting eye, grit, intensity, and play in the clutch.

Heinsohn was named coach of the Celtics in 1969. He led the team to two championships (1974 and 1976), and notched 427 victories before becoming a broadcaster in the 1980s.

Big Man Bill

Explaining Bill Russell to someone who never saw him play is impossible, because there is no contemporary frame of reference. Not physically. Not emotionally. Not intellectually.

"He is the first person who ever dominated his team sport without being the offensive guy," contends Bill Walton, who himself knew one or two things about playing championship basketball. "He was also instrumental in forcing everyone to treat athletes with individual dignity."

The Celtics won their first championship in 1957. They won their 11th in 1969. There was but one constant during those 13 seasons, and that constant was Bill Russell.

DOWN BY 21 IN THE FOURTH, CELTS WIN

*T*here was absolutely no reason to think it was possible. The Boston Celtics were down 21 points with one quarter left to play and their star, Paul Pierce, had missed 12 of his 14 shots. Boston's defense, the pulse of its basketball team, was weak, and barely detectable amid the groans of a capacity FleetCenter crowd that could not bear to watch the New Jersey Nets pummel their beloved franchise for another second.

Boston trailed, 74-53, and was about to relinquish home court advantage in this critical Game 3 of the 2002 Eastern Conference finals.

The Celtics simply could not win this basketball game.

But buoyed by an emotional plea by forward Antoine Walker, the Celtics submitted the single most incredible fourth-quarter performance in playoff history, ripping a sure victory from New Jersey's hands with a spectacular, improbable, truly unimaginable 94-90 win.

Nobody in NBA history had ever come back from a 21-point deficit in the final quarter of a playoff game.

As coach Jim O'Brien turned to his players in the huddle and began to give them instructions for the final 12 minutes, Walker, the co-captain, interjected.

"I cut him off," Walker would confess later. "I had to. I saw some things. I saw New Jersey over there smiling, and laughing, and the game wasn't even over.

WHO	**CELTICS** VS **NETS.**
WHERE	**FLEET CENTER, BOSTON.**
WHEN	**MAY 25, 2002.**
WHY THE DRAMA	With his team trailing 74-53 before the start of the fourth quarter, Antoine Walker challenged his teammates to show they would not be humiliated.

As security fought to restrain fans pushing toward the court, Antoine Walker leaped onto the scorer's table right in front of them. He pounded his chest and shouted, "That's heart."

That's also grandstanding, the Nets would later point out, and it didn't sit well with Jason Kidd and company. Humiliated and fired up, New Jersey won the series in 6. But we'll always have Game 3.

"I looked right at Paul, and I told him he wasn't playing his kind of basketball. He wasn't aggressive, and he was settling for jump shots.

"I looked at our team, and I told them we needed to send New Jersey a message. Even if we didn't win the game, we needed to show them something to carry over to Game 4.

Pierce proceeded to score 19 of his team's 41 fourth-quarter points on a series of would-not-be-denied drives to the basket. Kenny Anderson, who was 3 for 10 up to this point, stepped up and knocked down the jumpers New Jersey had dared him to make all day. Then there was Rodney Rogers, abysmal in the first two games against New Jersey, sinking six consecutive pressure free throws with the game on the line.

Left: Paul Pierce didn't even need to ask for crowd support when he and Antoine Walker (pounding his chest in the photo at right) led the NBA's biggest fourth-quarter comeback.

In the midst of this surreal turn-around, the FleetCenter crowd achieved such a frenzy that O'Brien couldn't even hear instructions from his assistants sitting directly beside him.

"It was so impressive to be in a building where nobody leaves," the coach marveled. "The team was down 26 (in the third quarter) and nobody leaves."

In the final 4:07 of the game, the New Jersey Nets did not score a single basket. Their only points in that final stretch were a pair of free throws from Jason Kidd.

It is impossible to overstate the magnitude of this resurrection, of this display of heart, and guts and intensity.

Even Michael Jordan never did what Walker and the Boston Celtics did in this game —defying the Nets, defying history, defying the longest of odds. That doesn't happen on skill alone. You need faith, hope, and a heart that beats like thunder. ❖

A CELTICS-LAKERS FIGHT TO THE FINISH

Fans knew it was going to be a good season for the Celtics when venerable Red Auerbach announced that this would be his farewell cigar.

And so it was that in the heat of the midnight hour, at the conclusion of the NBA's first year using an expanded playoff format, the Celtics waved Flag No. 15 with a dramatic Game 7 victory over the Los Angeles Lakers. It was the 113th contest of an 8 ½-month season, a campaign that captured the heads and hearts of New Englanders as never before.

"This is sweeter than our first championship [vs. Houston in 1981] because we beat a team that is equal to us," said Cedric Maxwell, who was heroic in the 111-102 finale with 24 points, 8 rebounds, and 8 assists.

Larry Bird (20 points, 12 rebounds) was the consensus series MVP, but in Game 7, Max was The Man. He scored 17 in a stellar first half that had seven early lead changes before it ended with the Celtics out in front, 58-52.

By then, both teams knew better than to ease up in this twisting series.

In Game 2, the Lakers had been in position to win when Gerald Henderson stole a James Worthy pass and tied the game. The Lakers had one last possession, but Magic Johnson used it to dribble out the clock. Boston went on to win in overtime.

Then in Game 4, after completely dominating the Celtics in the previous matchup, the Lakers were rolling toward a 3-1 series lead when Kevin McHale took down Kurt Rambis. The Celtics found new resolve in the moment, and Larry Bird and Robert Parish made big plays down the stretch. Meanwhile Magic botched some free throws and made a costly miscue; the Celtics won in overtime, again, to regain the home-court advantage.

Game 7 was hardly in the bag at halftime, and it still wasn't a done deal even at the end of the third quarter, when green lightning struck. With Bird sitting on the pine, the Celtics went on a 9-0 run for a 91-78 lead heading into the fourth quarter in the steamy (90-degree) Garden. As the period ended, Bird (who hit only 6 of 18 shots) was leading the cheers with M.L. Carr.

Above: M.L. Carr, Dennis Johnson, and Larry Bird led the cheers (Bird had to do something while he was hitting only 6 of 18 shots) even as Los Angeles threatened to rebound from a large deficit. Bird's towel dance must have done the trick, because Boston held on for yet another NBA championship banner.

Basketball

WHO	**CELTICS** VS. **LAKERS.**
WHERE	**BOSTON GARDEN.**
WHEN	**JUNE 12, 1984.**
WHY THE DRAMA	This series had everything, including a 97-degree Garden steam-bath win that put the Celts up 3-2. In Game 7, the lid blew off for good.

In 1984, Danny Ainge came off the bench to help Boston beat LA in one of the best NBA Finals. Later, the 3-point shooter extraordinaire became executive director of basketball operations for the Celtics.

But the gallant Lakers would not fold. A series that will be ranked with the NBA's best could not close with a blowout.

After Dennis Johnson (22 points) hit two free throws to give the Celtics their biggest lead (99-85 with 7:58 left), Kareem Abdul-Jabbar, Michael Cooper, and Magic led the Lakers back to within three points.

The Celtics could have panicked when their lead wilted to 105-102 with less than a minute to go. Not this year.

"I wasn't worried," Bird said. "That's when teams choke up; but as long as you have the lead, you should be OK."

LA's last chance to close to within one point ended when Parish blocked an off-balance Magic drive with 50 seconds left. DJ hit two huge free throws, and the Lakers, trailing by 107-102

with 45 seconds left, called time. Crowd control was a problem from that point on.

After the pause, McHale got the rebound off a second shot by LA and kicked it upcourt. Bird was fouled with 26 seconds left and made both. That sealed it. A pair of free throws by Bird set the final score, and Celtic glory was spread around like one cold beer among friends. ❖

Peter May, Globe Staff, contributed to this report.

LARRY VS. DOMINIQUE:
A GAME 7 SHOOTOUT

For Boston basketball fans, there is no memory quite like that of Larry Bird and Dominique Wilkins waging an epic final-quarter battle in the deciding game of the 1988 Eastern Conference semifinals at the Garden.

"We were sitting on the bench and saying it was like the shootout at the old corral," recalled then-rookie Celtic Reggie Lewis.

Dominique was great, scoring 16 in the fourth. Larry was greater, scoring 20 — on 9 of 10 shooting — and carrying the Celtics into the conference finals for a final time.

But how many people remember the game in its entirety? How it started out brilliantly, never had a single dead spot and wound up with the teams combining to shoot 59 percent with — get this — 15 total turnovers. How about Doc Rivers and his 16 points and 18 assists? Or Kevin McHale's 33 points, 13 rebounds and 4 blocks? Or Randy Wittman shooting 11 for 13 — all patented mid-range jumpers.

'Nique was sizzling from the start and would wind up with 47. Bird? He was just a so-so performer (by his lofty standards) until the fourth. That's when he slipped on the cloak with the red "S" and starting dropping in baskets at a 90 percent clip — baskets that were all mandatory because 'Nique was right with him.

In one unforgettable exchange, the two swapped baskets three times in the span of 1:23. Bird had the last say with a dagger-in-the-heart three right in front of the Atlanta bench, then a lefty drive. In the end, Bird totaled 34 points and the Celtics prevailed 118-116.

Was it the greatest Bird game? You crazy? Did Julia Child rate the greatest souffles?

Bird's teammate, Dirk Minniefield, concluded. "It was like he was playing on Mt. Olympus and we were all down on the Greek Islands."

Bird himself had a slightly simpler explanation. "Hell," he said, "this is my building."

Larry always talked that way because he always honestly believed he would be good. He had put in the hours, had taken the hundreds and thousands of jump shots and had stayed at the gym long after everyone else had gone home.

Looking back at the matchup with Wilkins, was it the greatest Bird game? You crazy? Did Julia Child rate the greatest souffles?

But the 1988 shootout was as good a mano a mano duel as the NBA playoffs have ever seen. At the start of its spectacular fourth quarter, "they each put their teams on their backs and said, 'Let's go,' " said Atlanta coach Mike Fratello. ❖

EASTERN CONFERENCE SEMIFINALS/ GAME 7

WHO	**CELTICS** VS **HAWKS.**
WHERE	**BOSTON GARDEN.**
WHEN	**MAY 22, 1988.**
WHY THE DRAMA	Two basketball superstars locked in a classic battle of one-upsmanship… loser goes home.

A closer look at the game

	Larry Bird	Dominique Wilkins
Min	47	43
FG	15-24	19-33
FA	3-3	8-9
Reb	4	5
A	6	3
F	2	0
Pts	34	47

It was as good a duel as the NBA playoffs have ever seen. Dominique Wilkins had 16 of his 47 in the fourth quarter. Larry Bird trumped him by shooting 9 for 10 and scoring 20 of his 34 in the 12 minutes as the Celts won, 118-116.

In one phenomenal stretch, they matched hoops on six consecutive possessions, three for Larry and three for 'Nique. Larry had the left hand going for three of the baskets (a banked scoop, a jumper, and a lefty drive) and he also found a streaking Danny Ainge for a 50-foot lefty touchdown pass.

The Bird summation: "To me, that was a one-quarter game. I really hadn't played well until that point. I remember stealing the ball a couple of times and getting some open jumpers to get my rhythm going."

He got it going all right. And Celts fans thrilled to every beat.

NCAA MADNESS AT THE GARDEN

They were too young to worry about the weight of expectation or the heartbreak of losing. With the 2006 women's basketball national championship hanging in the balance, the Maryland Terrapins rested their hopes on a starting lineup that featured a junior, two sophomores, and two freshmen, including a freshman point guard fueled by so much nerve that she calmly launched a 3-point bomb with the game on the line, even though she was 5 of 16 from the floor when she let it fly.

Kristi Toliver's shot over the outstretched arms of 6-foot-7-inch Duke center Alison Bales with 6.1 seconds left in regulation erased what had seemed an ominous 70-67 deficit and sent the game into overtime. The stunning fadeaway trey ignited a celebration among the Maryland players at center court that made you want to check the score twice. Had they won? Nah, they were just acting like it.

Over by their bench, the Duke players looked as though somebody had just driven off with their daddy's shiny new Cadillac.

Asked if there was any doubt they would win once they got the game into overtime, Maryland freshman Marissa Coleman said, "Not at all. Once Kristi hit that shot, we got into our huddle and said, `Overtime is our time.' "

Indeed, the 78-75 thriller at Boston's TD Banknorth Garden enabled the Terps to finish the season a perfect 6-0 in overtime, including a cliffhanger over Boston College in January. And they always did it with the kids playing a huge role.

Of course, Toliver's three from the right corner topped the charts in terms of dramatics.

"Big-time players want the shot in the big games," Toliver said. "So I wanted to take the shot. I knew if I could get it over [Bales], it felt pretty good. I knew as soon as it left my hands it was going in."

Toliver also figured heavily in the extra period, when the Blue Devils, clinging to a 75-74 lead with 34.2 seconds left, sent her to the line for the first time all night. The kid hit 'em both.

College

WHO	**MARYLAND** VS. **DUKE.**
WHERE	**TD BANKNORTH GARDEN,** BOSTON.
WHEN	**APRIL 4, 2006.**
WHY THE DRAMA	They were young. They were behind. And still they were some of the coolest hands ever to dismantle a Duke team in overtime

What about Connecticut?

Yeah, we know. UConn is New England's March Madness powerhouse franchise in both men's and women's basketball. The men are even coached by a Braintree, Massachusetts native (Jim Calhoun), who got his start at Northeastern.

But UConn represents the Nutmeg State, whereas this book is all about the Bay State, and we have our hands full just concentrating on thrillers that either happened here or happened to involve teams from around here.

That's why we chose a recent overtime stunner at the Garden as our March Madness moment, even knowing that this might not sit right with southern New England Huskies fans. And we expect we might also get flak from some locals who remember the triumphant Holy Cross men's team of 1947 (still the only Massachusetts team to win college basketball's biggest dance), or Northeastern's tragic 1982 triple-overtime loss to Villanova (76-72), or scrappy UMass's near take down of Kentucky in 1996 (later wiped from official record thanks to Marcus Camby's violation of NCAA rules on gift-taking).

We still think the ladies of Maryland deserve this spot. And hey, their season included a dramatic overtime win against BC, so they must be exceptional.

Above: Maryland freshman Marissa Coleman couldn't wait to celebrate with her teammates after they surprised the Duke Blue Devils in overtime.
Left: Kristi Toliver got off the clutch game-tying shot for Maryland, even though she was being defended by Duke's 6-foot-7-inch star center, Alison Bales.

Twenty-one seconds later, another freshman, Coleman, who buried a number of huge jumpers during Maryland's second-half comeback, found herself at the line with Maryland in front, 76-75. Coleman also had not taken a free throw all night.

But she hit 'em both, too.

The sting of losing is always painful. But the Duke Blue Devils flew back home knowing they blew a 13-point lead to a bunch of newcomers who

should have been nervous, or rattled, or at least humble, but chose to be none of those things.

Duke coach Gail Goestenkors shook her head sadly when asked if she was surprised by the clutch performance of the first-year Maryland players.

"No," she said. "I've seen it too many times," her team having split four games with the Terps this season. "I've seen instances where the pressure was really on and they've come through." ❖

TRIPLE OVERTIME AND NO CUP TO SHOW FOR IT

STANLEY CUP FINALS / GAME 1

The Bruins were going to lose. No, wait a minute, they were going to win.

The Boston Garden's lights were going to go out. They were going to pop like cannons on the Esplanade for the Fourth of July. No, they were going to burn in perpetuity, the eternal vapor lights of Causeway Street.

The MBTA was going to stop service at 12:30 a.m. on the dot, the way the MBTA always does things. No, the MBTA was going to run all night, all morning, until every last token in the Commonwealth was collected and until no one would dare ask again if the mythical and long-lost Charlie would ever return.

The Bruins and Edmonton Oilers shared a line in the Stanley Cup record book after they skated, plodded and tobogganed their way into triple overtime in Game 1 of the 1990 Stanley Cup finals. In the end, the Bruins lost, 3-2, on Petr Klima's goal at 55:13 of overtime (logged at 1:22 a.m.), capping the longest game in finals history. (Note that this was not the longest game in Bruins playoff history, which includes a six-overtime first-round loss to Toronto, 1-0, on April 3, 1933, at 104:46 of OT.).

For one protracted and schizophrenic evening/morning, the Oilers, the Bruins, and a sellout crowd of 14,448 lived through the highs, lows and hit posts of one of the Garden's most memorable events. Finally, Klima settled it, vacating his spot at the remote end of the Oiler bench to fire a shot by Andy Moog from the right faceoff circle.

Way back in the third period it was legendary defenseman Ray Bourque who revived the Bruins with a pair of late goals. Then in the overtimes, countless good scoring opportunities were had by both teams but turned back by Moog and his Oiler counterpart, Bill Ranford.

The Garden's vapor lights, which take approximately 15 minutes to reach full power once switched on, automatically turned off at 12:33 a.m., with the third OT only 2:41 old. The lights were close to overheating after nearly six hours of operation. But they, and the game, were back on at 12:58 a.m.

Not long before the great vapor failure, Garden PA man Joel Perlmutter had announced that the MBTA's last train would depart at 12:30. Later, he came back on to say that the trains would run all night. His most memorable announcement, though, came at the game's conclusion: "Good night . . . and good morning, everyone," he said. ❖

Nancy L. Marrapese and Marvin Pave, Globe Staff, contributed to this report.

WHO	**BRUINS** VS. **OILERS.**
WHERE	**BOSTON GARDEN**, BOSTON.
WHEN	**MAY 15, 1990.**
WHY THE DRAMA	Boston went into the finals with home ice and great confidence. Edmonton set them straight in this marathon dogfight.

RAY BOURQUE: "The Captain" played his part in Game 1 scoring two goals in the third period that propelled the B's into overtime. This was nothing new for the Bruins' all-time leader in points, assists, and games. No one bled black and gold like Bourque. The NHL says his 20-plus seasons with the Bruins is the longest stint with one team by any professional athlete.

CAM NEELY: "The Great No. 8" was held scoreless in the 1990 Cup, ironic for the B's all-time leading playoff goal scorer. The prototypical forward, Neely mixed undying tenacity with dead-on shooting. In 1993-'94 he racked up 50 goals in 44 games, an ultimate NHL achievement. Deeply embedded in the Boston landscape, Neely is considered the iconic Bruin of his generation.

What Happened Next
Missing Mr. Neely

The 55 regular-season goals, the playoff victories he helped fuel over Hartford, Montreal, and Washington, and the Bruins' rush to the Stanley Cup finals all faded away quickly for Cam Neely when the Oilers won the 1990 trophy in five games. Neely had 12 playoff goals, but none versus Edmonton.

BC CRACKS THE FROZEN FOUR

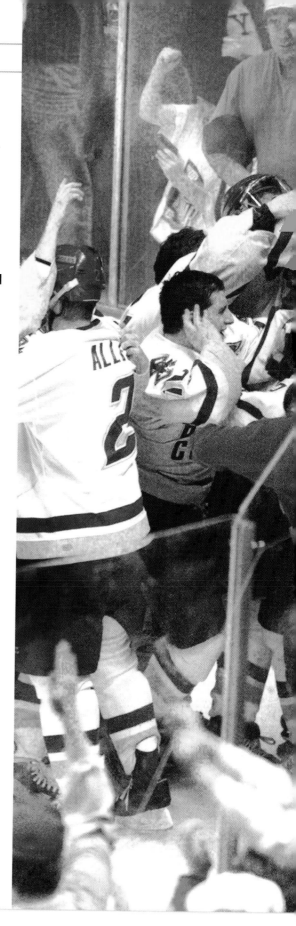

The Zambonis were just about threatening to run them over and NCAA officials were trying to usher them away from the maelstrom at Pepsi Arena, but the Boston College hockey players were having none of it.

Nobody tells the national champions what to do. This was their ice, their time, their wood-and-gold trophy, and they weren't about to let any of it go.

This wasn't arrogance, it was catharsis. So the Eagles frolicked and cavorted and embraced and smiled for pictures in front of disposable cameras and just generally enjoyed being liberated. Forty-five minutes after Krys Kolanos's goal at 4:43 of overtime beat resilient North Dakota, 3-2, in the 2001 NCAA final at the Albany, New York arena, they were trying to stretch the euphoria into forever.

Pick a disparaging frame of reference — 52 years, four years, four minutes — and Kolanos's goal killed it.

It gave the Eagles their second national crown, their first since 1949. "Now people will be quiet about it," said freshman Chuck Kobasew, the tournament MVP.

It enabled the Class of 2001 to enjoy its first success after three straight futile Frozen Fours. "Hey, perseverance pays off," said defenseman Bobby Allen.

But first, North Dakota almost pulled it out after trailing heading into the third period just as it had the year before.

With less than five minutes to go in the third period, the Eagles seemed in control, 2-0, courtesy of second-period goals by Kobasew (from Jeff Giuliano) and by Mike Lephart, whose shot deflected in off a defenseman. That lead loomed huge because BC goalie Scott Clemmensen was playing the game of his life, making 34 saves, including a piece de resistance near the end of the first period when he reached behind him with his glove and robbed Bryan Lundbohm of a certain score.

Then came the late collapse, and it was as unforeseen as it was deflating.

BC was called for having too many men on the ice when Tony Voce jumped over the boards while Brian Gionta was by the bench reaching for a new stick. North Dakota coach Dean Blais took a chance and pulled his goalie early, and it paid off when North Dakota scored with 3:42 left. Then with less than a minute remaining, a tipped shot eluded Clemmensen to tie it.

"We got kind of down heading off the ice, and rightly so," said Jerry York, the unassuming, paternal coach who had raised the program from the rubble since coming to the Heights seven years earlier.

But they got back up, and eventually the Eagles prevailed on what Kolanos called "my bread and butter. It was quick transition. Voce gave me the puck, I put a deke on the D, and then went wide."

Thus BC achieved vindication, validation, and vengeance. Their title march first included paybacks to two of the teams that had knocked them out of the three previous Frozen Fours — Maine and Michigan. The victory over North Dakota made them three for three. ❖

Left: It might look like a brawl, but this is just what happens when a Boston College team finally gets a chance to celebrate winning a national championship.
Right: Enter the man of the hour, Krys Kolanos, who knocked in the winning goal in overtime.

College

HOCKEY / NCAA CHAMPIONSHIP

WHO	**BOSTON COLLEGE** VS. **NORTH DAKOTA.**
WHERE	**PEPSI ARENA,** ALBANY, NEW YORK.
WHEN	**APRIL 7, 2001.**
WHY THE DRAMA	As BC blew a late lead and headed to overtime, the ghost of three straight futile Frozen Fours hovered ominously. Then came Krys Kolanos, ghost buster.

At the end of the long bus ride home after BC's glorious victory, the Eagles arrived at their destination with a light rain falling and an enormous salute raging. Despite the late (early?) hour, despite the weather, almost 400 people had massed outside Conte Forum to welcome home, and serenade, the group that had ended BC's 52-year wait for its second national title.

NORTHEASTERN STEALS THE BEANPOT

The **1980 Beanpot was the best of the best. It was David,** without a slingshot, against Goliath I and II. It was Cinderella. It was an improbable dream. If it hadn't happened, many would say it couldn't have happened.

Northeastern was David, Boston University was Goliath I, and Boston College was Goliath II. The Huntington Hounds, who hadn't won the Beanpot in their first 27 tries, entered the tournament with a paltry 3-11 record. BU was 9-8, and BC (17-4-1) was the favorite. Northeastern, a.k.a. the Consolation Kids, looked like an automatic first-game victim.

Right: Northeastern's improbable win triggered a celebratory ride for coach Fernie Flaman.
Below: Wayne Turner's overtime goal capped the Huskies' tournament triumph, and wrote the perfect ending to this Beanpot Cinderella story.

HOCKEY / BEANPOT FINALS

WHO	BOSTON COLLEGE VS. NORTHEASTERN.
WHERE	BOSTON GARDEN.
WHEN	FEBRUARY 4, 1980.
WHY THE DRAMA	When David beats Goliath in overtime, well, that's a nice little story. But when two Goliaths fall in overtime, the story must be writ large.

For more than half a century on the first two Mondays in February, Boston University, Boston College, Harvard University, and Northeastern University have battled for the Beanpot. What began as a simple little hockey tournament quickly grew into a revered winter event that defies practical measurement. Highlights include a decade of heavyweight BC-Harvard showdowns, long stretches of BU dominance, and Northeastern triumphing after 27 years of futility.

Two more Pot boilers

Northeastern hockey coach Bruce Crowder had called Boston University the New York Yankees of the Beanpot. Sure enough, the 2005 Terriers matched their hardball counterparts with their 26th crown on Chris Bourque's overtime goal. BU, which defeated Northeastern 3-2, showed once again why it is the little local tournament's lone empire.

BU's Sean Fields did everything but pull a rabbit out of the water bottle that rested on top of his goal. Fans at the 2004 Beanpot were treated to some truly unbelievable saves even though, unfortunately, his scintillating act lacked a perfect ending. Despite Fields's heroics, Boston College won its 13th Beanpot, 2-1, on Ty Hennes's tying goal late in regulation and Ryan Murphy's overtime game-winner.

Not this time.

The hockey gods smiled on the lunch-pail gang. The Huskies, who were the biggest underdog in tournament history, roared and beat both Goliaths in overtime.

Many Huskies were heroes those two Monday nights, but none more than a diminutive savior from Western Canada.

Wayne Turner, the former fiery right wing from Kitimat, British Columbia, scored an overtime goal just a few ticks before midnight to win the final on a tumultuous night at the Boston Garden. Many in attendance swore the old building never swayed as it did that night.

"You know, I don't recall hearing all the noise," Turner said. "I know it was there, but I don't think I heard it all because of all the commotion we were making. What I felt was just great. We won the Beanpot for the first time."

Turner's goal gave Northeastern a 5-4 win over Boston College. Even diehard Eagles fans couldn't be too disappointed. He made the have-not Huskies the haves.

"It all happened so quick," said Turner. "There was a faceoff in our zone, and we won. I broke up ice. Dale Ferdinandi got the puck and sort of fell and got the puck to me. I just shot high to the goalie's glove side, which was on my right. It went in."

The pass was intended for Larry Parks. Ferdinandi was tripped going into the BC zone. Parks overskated the feed and it ended up on Turner's stick.

Turner had actually already earned a hero tag the previous week. Northeastern avoided its usual spot in the third-place game by beating BU, 6-5. After scoring a second-period goal, Turner assisted on the winning tally by John Montgomery of Gloucester. Massachusetts, and sent the Huskies to only their third Beanpot final. ❖

FOUR GOALS IN UNDER A MINUTE

They packed the place.

It was a winter night in 1970… Ridge Arena in Braintree, Massachusetts… people stuffed in every corner, filling the balcony.

They came to see Robbie Ftorek play hockey.

It was the 16th game of a perfect season for Needham High School, the defending state champions. Walpole was the only team to beat Needham the previous season and the rink was rocking.

With about a minute and a half left in the game, Walpole scored to take a 3-1 lead. The Rebel bench exploded, players jumping onto the ice to celebrate, throwing their gloves into the air and into the stands.

In the minutes it took to restore order, Ftorek skated back to the goal to talk to his dejected sophomore goalie, Cap Raeder.

"How many you want?" he said.

"Huh?" said Raeder.

"How many do you want?" Ftorek repeated, jabbing his finger into Raeder's chest.

"Just get enough to win."

In 52 seconds, Ftorek and his mates scored four goals, the last into an empty net, to pull off a miraculous 5-3 victory. They went on to repeat as state champions and post an undefeated season.

"It was like magic," said Raeder, now a professional hockey scout.

So magical that nobody really recalls the exact number or nature of goals scored by Ftorek, other than that he was right in the middle of everything.

"All I can remember is bang-bang-bang-bang, we win," said former Ftorek wingman and longtime St. Sebastian's hockey coach Steve Dagdigian years later. "I can still see [Walpole star and future NHL fixture Mike] Milbury hanging out at the food stand afterward, shaking his head."

Ftorek went on to play hockey at all the higher levels. His US Olympic team shocked the hockey world by claiming a silver medal in Sapporo, Japan, in 1972. Later he signed with Detroit, then he jumped to the Phoenix Roadrunners of the fledgling World Hockey Association in 1974, scoring a career-high 117 points (46 goals) in 1976 and earning league MVP honors.

When Phoenix folded, he moved to Cincinnati and then Quebec. In 1979, the NHL absorbed the WHA, and Ftorek stayed on with the Nordiques, serving as team captain. He finished his playing career with the New York Rangers, then he dove right into a successful coaching career highlighted by a 76-65-14 stretch at the helm of the Bruins.

But it was those wondrous high school days that New Englanders remember best. It was the peak of hockey in Boston, with the Bruins winning Stanley Cups and every kid in town clamoring for skates and a patch of ice. Even then, Ftorek stood head and shoulders above the rest. ❖

John Powers, Globe Staff, contributed to this report.

Right: Needham High School hockey legend Robbie Ftorek routinely dazzled Boston-area sports fans back in the day. His unparalleled skills led the Needham squad to two state titles at Boston Garden. And that was just the beginning of Ftorek's rise.

HOCKEY / FINAL GAME OF THE REGULAR SEASON

WHO	**NEEDHAM** VS. **WALPOLE**.
WHERE	**RIDGE ARENA,** BRAINTREE, MASSACHUSETTS.
WHEN	**WINTER, 1970.**
WHY THE DRAMA	At a time when the Big Bad Bruins were still must-see TV, high school legend Robbie Ftorek found a way to steal the show.

Ftorek the Great

His first skates came with toe picks.

Robbie Ftorek began as a figure skater, tutored by Maribel Vinson Owen, the fabled mother-hen coach who perished in the 1961 plane crash in Belgium that wiped out the US team. So when he laced on hockey skates, Ftorek found himself well ahead of the curve.

"I already knew about edges and leverage," he told the Globe's John Powers in 2001. "So they were always teaching me something else."

By the time he made the Needham High varsity, Ftorek had already mastered college-level courses in stick handling and passing and shooting.

"Occasionally you'd think, how does he do that?" says Steve Dagdigian, Ftorek's wingman at Needham. "He would always have something in his bag of tricks."

He was The Great 8 (Fleming Mackell's number with the Bruins) and magic seemed to follow him around the rink. The legendary 1970 game, when Ftorek led a four-goal comeback against Mike Milbury's Walpole team with barely a minute to play, seems incredible, but it's been backed up by fabled Needham goalie Cap Raeder.

"It sounds like a Babe Ruth thing," acknowledged Raeder. "But it happened."

Historical footnote: Milbury, who'd broken a skate just before the comeback, played the rest of the game wearing a teammate's boot. "Had I had two good skates on, it never would have happened," he said, laughing.

WHEN NANCY MET OKSANA (AND TONYA)

In the end, it was not about the Olympic gold medal, which Nancy Kerrigan lost to Ukrainian teenager Oksana Baiul by the slimmest margin possible: the tiebreaking artistic mark on one judge's card. It was about resilience, relief, and redemption.

The only judge who counted at the 1994 Olympics in Hamar, Norway was the one in Nancy Kerrigan's head. Only Kerrigan knew what she was capable of in that moment, and what she'd been through in the past 11 months. And when the music stopped, she professed to have won the gold medal that mattered most to her.

"For me, in my heart, in my mind, I did, yes," said Kerrigan after she'd earned a silver medal to go along with the bronze she won at Albertville two years ago. "I was enjoying myself and I did the elements. How can I complain?"

She might have had the official gold too, except that what matters in figure skating is who has the most first-place votes. Baiul had five, Kerrigan four. Baiul prevailed because Jan Hoffmann, who won the silver medal for East Germany in 1980, gave her a 5.9 artistic mark to Kerrigan's 5.8. Though Hoffmann's total marks for both skaters were equal, the artistic mark is the tiebreaker in the long program.

Still, seven weeks before, when Kerrigan sat screaming in a corridor after an assailant linked to teammate Tonya Harding clubbed her landing knee, it seemed unlikely that the Stoneham, Massachusetts, skater would even make it back to Olympus, much less make the awards podium again.

"I was really proud of myself," said Kerrigan after she'd landed five triple jumps, three of them in combinations. "To watch the American flag raised for the efforts that I've put in to be here — it's thrilling."

Yet most of the skating people in the building felt the American flag should have been on top. "I thought the order of the top two should have been reversed," said Louis Stong, who coaches Canada's Josee Chouinard. "Kerrigan's program was cleaner, less posed and had more skating."

Kerrigan's program included two tough combination jumps — a triple toe/triple toe and a triple salchow/double toe. Baiul's had only one combination — a double axel/double toe — and she tossed it in during the final seconds when she realized she'd lose without it.

THE ICE FOLLIES:

It was the whack heard 'round the world. "Why?" cried Nancy Kerrigan after a baton-wielding stranger hit her above the right knee at a skating competition in Detroit. It turned out that her assailant had been hired by Jeff Gillooly, husband of competitor Tonya Harding. Kerrigan went on to win the silver medal at the Olympics. Gillooly went to prison. Harding went nowhere, unless you consider court appearances and celebrity boxing a step up.

Above: Despite all the controversies, silver medalist Nancy Kerrigan (right) found her smile when she joined gold medal winner Oksana Baiul on the Olympic podium.

Olympics

WHO	**NANCY KERRIGAN, OKSANA BAIUL, TONYA HARDING,** ET AL.
WHERE	**HAMAR,** NORWAY.
WHEN	**FEBRUARY 25, 1994.**
WHY THE DRAMA	Can you think of another time when a practice collision, a broken boot lace, and a knee-clubbing figured into one Olympic skating event?

TENLEY'S TURN

As soap-opera sensational as the women's figure skating competition was in 1994, it wasn't the first time that an Olympian from the Boston area found herself starring in a melodrama on ice. Remember 1956, the year of Newton native Tenley Albright?

Albright, who had already overcome a bout of childhood polio to capture a silver medal at the 1952 Olympics, was world champion and the clear favorite coming into the 1956 Games. Then she spiked herself in practice less than two weeks before opening ceremonies, slashing her right ankle to the bone. Albright's surgeon father was able to strap the ankle so she could walk on it, but she was unable to practice, and not until the day before the competition did she try her jumps, with mixed results.

Luckily, Albright didn't have to do any triple-triple jump combinations, because at that point skating was mostly about school figures meant to test precision, poise, and patience. Still, rising above adversity during Olympic competition takes a special breed of courage, and Albright did her home city proud when she became the first American woman to win a gold medal in the sport.

Though Kerrigan doubled her planned triple flip, she landed it cleanly. Baiul two-footed hers. Yet when the marks came up, Baiul had won the votes of the judges from Poland, Czech Republic, Ukraine, China and (East) Germany. The Communist bloc may have broken up geographically, but it lives on in the rink.

Kerrigan had the judges' sympathy for her ordeal, but so did Baiul, a virtual orphan whose mother is dead and whose father disappeared when she was a toddler. And after a frightening practice collision with Germany's Tanja Szewczenko left her with stitches in her shin and a sore back and shoulder, Baiul felt fortunate to skate at all in the final.

When the marks went up, Baiul began weeping. By then, Kerrigan was already in the dressing room, her private gold medal won. ❖

OUTKICKED, BUT STILL QUEEN OF THE POOL

Seven times previously we'd seen it at Olympus: Jenny Thompson launches herself from the relay blocks and comes home with a gold medal for everybody. Twice at Barcelona in 1992. Twice at Atlanta in 1996. Three times at Sydney in 2000.

So at the Athens Games, when the Danvers, Massachusetts native began the anchor leg of the 4 x 100-meter freestyle with a lead of nearly four-10ths of a second, everybody in the pool figured the Yanks were good as gold again. At least, they did until Australia's Jodie Henry outkicked Thompson decisively to lead her mates to a world record (3 minutes 35.94 seconds). In so doing she handed the US its first loss in the race since 1988 and only its second since 1956.

"It was a change of pace for me to be passed by that much," said Thompson, who still sparked her team to an American record (3:36.39) that was more than two-10ths faster than their winning time in 2000. "Usually it's the other way around."

But the 31-year-old Thompson wasn't quite as dominant as in her younger days. Four of her countrywomen were faster in the 100 freestyle at trials the month before the Olympics. Ordinarily, that would have made her a prelim swimmer in the 400 free relay, but her career record demanded that the coaches put her in the anchorwoman position.

"I think my experience did have a lot to do with their final decision," said Thompson, who had produced not just gold medals but world records in the last three 4 x 100 free relays at Olympus.

Thompson posted an excellent split (53.77); only Henry (a blistering 52.95), world record-holder Libby Lenton (53.57), and defending 100 free champion Inge de Bruijn of the Netherlands (53.37) were faster. "Jenny really put up a fight," conceded Australian coach Leigh Nugent. "Probably swam faster than we expected."

Just not fast enough. Still, it was the 11th Olympic medal for Thompson, who already held the record for most medals by an American woman in any sport and trailed only all-time leader Larissa Latynina, who won 18 for the Soviet Union in gymnastics.

"It doesn't feel that much different than 10," mused Thompson. "Whether it's 30 or 10, it's a lot of medals. I feel blessed being here. My fourth Olympics — not many people get to do that." ❖

Olympics

WOMEN'S SWIMMING /
4 X 100-METER FREESTYLE RELAY

WHO	**US** VS. **AUSTRALIA** AND OTHERS.
WHERE	**ATHENS, GREECE.**
WHEN	**AUGUST 14, 2004.**
WHY THE DRAMA	Everyone expected to see Jenny Thompson go out on top. Well, everyone but the Australians.

What Happened Next

Number 12

By the end of the Athens games, Thompson had medal number 12 (another silver) after swimming one last relay leg. Her 100 butterfly contribution completed yet another chapter of swimming history. It gave her one more medal than swimmers Mark Spitz and Matt Biondi and shooter Carl Osburn amassed during their Olympic careers. Thompson's Olympic dozen is the most by a US athlete in any sport.

Above: Year after year, Jenny Thompson was unbeatable in relays. She always pushed her teammates to Olympic gold. But perfection can't last forever.
Right: Thompson left the 2004 Games holding the overall record for most Olympic medals by any US athlete.

APRIL 7, 2002 ❱❱ BY MICHAEL VEGA, GLOBE STAFF

BOSTON'S OWN 'DUEL IN THE SUN'

At what many believe was the best-ever Boston Marathon men's race in 1982, Alberto Salazar and Dick Beardsley were gladiators in singlets and running shoes.

They were marathoners of iron will, single-minded determination and indefatigable spirit. But on that warm April day, the cocksure Salazar, 23, and the unassuming Beardsley, three years Salazar's senior, engaged in a dangerous game of brinkmanship.

They pushed each other over 26 grueling miles and 385 yards, raising the ante to the limit of human endurance. It resulted in an epic "Duel in the Sun" between Salazar and Beardsley, the closest finish in Boston Marathon history to that point. It ended with a dehydrated and fatigued Salazar summoning every ounce of strength in the final 150 yards to hold off a last-gasp kick by Beardsley.

Salazar, who was born in Cuba and raised in Wayland, Massachusetts, crossed the tape 1 1/2 steps ahead of Beardsley to finish his one and only Boston Marathon in 2 hours, 8 minutes, 52 seconds, a course record. Beardsley, the Minnesotan who trained under Greater Boston Track Club coach Bill Squires, ran the race of his life, hoping to press the issue in the Newton hills and bring Salazar to his knees with a series of surges. But Salazar never broke, and Beardsley, whose right hamstring cramped in the final mile but came unknotted by a fortuitous false step in a pothole near the Eliot Lounge, finished two seconds back.

Like a pair of punch-drunk prizefighters who had gone toe-to-toe for 15 rounds, Salazar and Beardsley fell into each other's arms at the finish near the Prudential Center.

Right: Alberto Salazar (left) was a step behind Dick Beardsley as the race passed through Brookline's Coolidge Corner in the final miles. That would change.

BOSTON MARATHON

WHO	**ALBERTO SALAZAR** VS. **DICK BEARDSLEY.**
WHERE	**HOPKINTON TO BOSTON.**
WHEN	**APRIL 19, 1982.**
WHY THE DRAMA	Neck and neck nearly the whole way, local favorite Salazar finally pulled ahead of Beardsley and won by just two seconds in a sprint to the tape.

One tough tradition

The sign in Hopkinton says, "It all starts here." What it ought to read, however, is: "Boston, the Alpha and Omega of Marathons."

It is a strand of eight shimmering pearls — Hopkinton, Ashland, Framingham, Natick, Wellesley, Newton, Brookline, and Boston — strung together by a 26-mile, 385-yard ribbon of asphalt.

When the Boston Athletic Association laid out the course in 1897, the intent was to duplicate the long-distance route Pheidippides followed on his fabled run from Marathon to Athens in 490 B.C. And so, from its start near Hopkinton Green at 490 feet above sea level to its rapid, 310-foot descent into Ashland to the surround-sound experience at Wellesley College to the unrelenting torture test of Heartbreak Hill to the breathless Back Bay finish on Boylston Street, the Boston Marathon has remained a time-honored test of human endurance.

Even Pheidippides, who dropped dead after completing his marathon trek to Athens, would have found Boston to be no walk in the Parthenon.

"I know I've never been so beaten up after a marathon as I was after Boston in 1982," Dick Beardsley told the Globe in 1990. "I don't think it was because it was the fastest 2:08:54 marathon I've ever run. I think the course just … took a lot out of me."

Above: The two runners stuck close and pushed each other over the entire length of Boston's incredibly grueling marathon course.
Above right: After he won, Salazar was taken to the medical tent to be treated for dehydration.

Salazar, who became dangerously dehydrated after taking, by his count, no more than 2 1/2 cups of water out on the course, saluted the man who very nearly buried him.

"Great race, man," said Salazar before being helped to the medical tent to have six liters of fluid pumped into his body. "You pushed me harder than anybody's ever pushed me in my life." The champion marathoner had lost 10 pounds from his already lean 145-pound frame.

"We almost put each other in the ground, seriously," remembered Beardsley. "I might not have had to go into the medical tent afterward, but I probably should've. I mean, I was so hammered.

"Neither one of us ever ran that fast again after that race."

Salazar came close. The 1982 Boston Marathon capped only the first half of an amazing year. He went on to engage in another epic duel, this time against Mexico's Rodolfo Gomez, in the New York City Marathon that fall. They entered the final mile in Central Park running side by side. After racing through a cloud of dust raised by police cruisers, Salazar emerged with the lead and won by four seconds in 2:09:29.

As it turned out, racing marathons was the easy part of Beardsley's life. He retired from it in 1988 and returned to Minnesota to take up dairy farming, a vocation that almost cost him his life in November 1989 when he was involved in an accident.

"I was unloading corn from a wagon up into a corn bin," Beardsley said. "I got my leg caught in the power take-off, which runs the auger, a long shaft that hooks back to the tractor and spins at 640 revolutions per minute.

"It just beat the living tar out of me, about tore off my left leg and broke my right arm and all my ribs on my right side and punctured my right lung."

It was only the first of many trials for the resilient Beardsley. In 1992 he was in an auto accident that left him with neck and back injuries, and in 1993, while running in a snowstorm, he was hit by a truck that did additional damage to his neck, back, and leg.

In dealing with all of these difficulties and more, Beardsley developed an addiction to painkillers. He was arrested Sept. 30, 1996, for forging prescriptions. He did community service and kicked his drug addiction after methadone treatment in 1997.

"The good Lord gave me the gift of being able to run; he gave me the gift of a positive attitude and a strong willpower," Beardsley said. "There are certain things willpower helps you through, like running." ❖

More Marathon drama

There were plenty of great Boston Marathons. The races, and the names connected with them, remain legendary scores of years later: Clarence DeMar, John McDermott, Johnny Miles, Leslie Pawson, Johnny Kelley, Tarzan Brown, Gerard Cote, Stylianos Kyriakides, Yun Bok Suh, Johnny Kelley the Younger, Eino Oksanen, Aurele Vandendriessche, Morio Shigematsu, Bill Rodgers.

The greatest is purely a matter of opinion. The popular choice has usually been Alberto Salazar's dramatic win over Dick Beardsley in 1982. But the words that appeared in the Globe account of Kenyan Ibrahim Hussein's wondrous 1988 triumph over Tanzanian Juma Ikangaa make a different case.

"It was over those final 600 yards that this Boston race separated itself from the rest. Even though (the Salazar-Beardsley duel) remains etched in memory, Hussein's calculated comeback to overtake Ikangaa with 120 yards to go and beat him to the tape by 1 second and less than three yards eclipsed it in terms of raw drama."

Maybe. It's certainly fun to debate, anyway.

BOSTON BILLY BARELY OUTRUNS THE FIELD

It was the best of all possible Marathon races and also the **worst.** It came complete with a Hollywood script and a wall-to-wall crowd scene over the final dozen miles that almost wrecked the production. More than a million people saw the race, most of them from grandstand seats in the middle of the road.

Below: Spectators crowded so close to Rodgers and the rest of the pack that they nearly turned the final miles into an obstacle course.

BOSTON MARATHON

Bill Rodgers, the homebred, won it by two seconds, barely getting to the tape in time. Texan Jeff Wells, whose presence was like a barber's breath on the leader's neck, had to out jostle 1) a cop, and 2) a placard-bearing demonstrator in the tumultuous 100 yards at the end. Rodgers, in 2 hours, 10 minutes, 13 seconds, missed his own course record by merely 18 seconds, and Wells missed winning the race by about from here to your TV set.

Of 4,212 who started, the first six finishers fled down the course on an ideal 46-degree day in less than 2:12. In order behind the Rodgers-Wells scene, they were Esa Tikkanen of Finland; 1976 winner Jack Fultz; Randy Thomas of Fitchburg, Massachusetts, in only his second Marathon; and Kevin Ryan of New Zealand. Frank Shorter, Olympic champ at Munich, finished 23rd, the ninth gold medalist to by stymied here.

Because the officials' bus was delayed en route, no clocking was recorded at the Coolidge Corner checkpoint for the first time in 82 years. Thus, we will never know how rapidly the effervescent Wells raced over the concluding 2.2 miles in his sensational charge at Rodgers. But Rodgers, who knew Wells was back there and on the drive, later remarked, "Worried? Of course I was worried. Jeff Wells is known for his big finish, and I'm not that strong at the end of a race. … Let's say that I was happy I got to the finish when I did."

It was closer than any Boston Marathon finish that preceded it.

But Wells, a 22-year-old seminary student, thinks the outcome was decided much earlier.

"My biggest disappointment is not my finish, but the fact I didn't get into the race soon enough," he said. "My goof was in letting Rodgers get out to a big lead early in the race."

At the halfway mark, 13 miles and some small change in Wellesley Square, the tough Texan was running in seventh position. He had strong visual contact with the leaders — Rodgers, Tikkanen and Ryan — but his deficit, 19 seconds, was formidable if the trio held up well over the final half of the foot race.

Rodgers broke from the pack at 17 ½ miles, then proceeded to race over the next two miles, including Heartbreak, in 20 minutes, 45 seconds — the swiftest hill run in 82 years. That aggressive attack captured the race for him.

Rodgers then ran the final 13 miles faster than any previous race winner (1:04:39), and it was an unconscious blessing because Wells was even faster in the flight in from Wellesley (1:04:22).

"I never had a harder race on a day that wasn't hot," Rodgers said. "I was always having to deal with a fast pace and a challenge from someone."

The final Wells bid came much closer than Rodgers's supporters could be comfortable with, but it confirmed their man's own fears. Rodgers candidly conceded that had it gone only a few yards longer, he might have lost a race he wanted very much to win. ❖

WHO	**BILL RODGERS** AND **JEFF WELLS.**
WHERE	**HOPKINTON TO BOSTON.**
WHEN	**APRIL 17, 1978.**
WHY THE DRAMA	Not known for his kick, Rodgers edged Wells by two seconds for his second victory in what was then the closest finish in Boston history.

The Globe identified him as "Will Rogers" when he won the Falmouth Road Race in 1974. In 1975, when he won his first Boston Marathon, the newspaper was closer, calling him "Will Rodgers." A few years later, Bill Rodgers had run so far so fast that he was known simply as "Boston Billy."

Rodgers won the Boston Marathon four times from 1975-80, won four consecutive New York Marathons from 1976-79, and won the 1977 Fukuoka International Marathon (which was considered the unofficial world championship).

UTA'S BRAVEST RUN

Uta Pippig, the darling of Boston, took three straight marathons and set a record 2:21:45 for the course in 1994. But it was her win at the race's centennial celebration in 1996 that has become part of marathon lore. There she was, coming down the home stretch battling apparent menstrual cramps, accompanied by blood and diarrhea that trickled down her legs. Undeterred, she pushed on, took the lead in the last mile and won.

She grimaces as she discusses the messy finish. English is her second language, and this former medical student from Germany struggles to find the right words. "There is no word in the English language for becoming famous for something bad happening to you," she says.

The media handled the subject of her "women's problems" delicately, referring obliquely to menstrual cramps. The crowd applauded her grit, and women everywhere sympathized and shuddered.

But they weren't cramps at all. In fact, she wasn't even having her period.

"I had severe colitis," she says. For three months before the marathon, she had trained intensely at high altitudes, and had an inflamed large intestine. It had "calmed down," but flared up again just before the race.

"I was very nervous. There was a lot of pressure. This would be my third straight win," she says. After the awards ceremony and press conference, she went straight to the hospital, where she stayed for four days. As for her public plight, she says: "At the time, I blocked it out as good as I could. I didn't want to disappoint my family, my coach, and my friends. It would be my third straight win, and I couldn't give up."

It can't be easy to stay the course when you are exposed in this manner before television cameras and hundreds of thousands of spectators. And then there's pain.

"After 4 miles, I was thinking several times to drop out because it hurt so much," she said. "But in the end, I won."

She won because she found something to keep her going after Heartbreak Hill, something that allowed her to make up a 220-meter deficit. And she won because Kenya's Tegla Loroupe developed leg cramps of her own and could not hold the lead.

The images are vivid. Running down Beacon Street, Pippig was gaining on Loroupe as the two raced toward Kenmore. Without breaking stride, Pippig grabbed a water bottle, ripped away the top with her teeth, then took a sip. She kept running and gulped again. She raised the bottle to her lips for one final drink, gaining ground with each step.

Her thirst quenched, Pippig spiked the bottle to the ground, then sped past Loroupe like a Miata passing an 18-wheeler. The folks near Kenmore roared. She had made up 30 seconds in less than a mile.

"It was amazing for me because so many people screamed even when it was not possible to win anymore," said Pippig. "They said, 'You can catch her.' And I said, 'Come on, guys, it is such a big gap.' It was like a connection between us and I just started fighting and I imagined I could fly."

Smiling through the pain, Pippig flew across the finish line. Then she did what she always does in Boston. She blew kisses. ❖

> **"It's a cool course. It's very challenging. It has a lot of character, with this one very unnecessary hill."**
> —UTA PIPPIG

BOSTON MARATHON

WHO	**UTA PIPPIG** VS. **TEGLA LOROUPE.**
WHERE	**HOPKINTON** TO **BOSTON.**
WHEN	**APRIL 15, 1996.**
WHY THE DRAMA	As if winning a marathon in the final mile isn't hard enough, Pippig did it while battling cramps and diarrhea. Now that's a champion.

What Happened Next

Unjustly accused

As an athlete for the East German government, Uta Pippig had been given various vitamins and supplements and "this and that," performance-enhancing substances that were banned from the sport. "They would give you things and you didn't know what they were," she says.

In 1986 she began training with Dieter Hogen, who agreed with her no-substance approach. But the banned substance issue would later dog her; in 1998, she was suspended from running for two years for failing a random drug test that revealed a ratio of testosterone-epitestosterone greater than that allowed by international standards.

Nearly four months after the suspension expired, Pippig reached a settlement with the federation stating that the ban was not legally justified, and it was removed from the record.

ROSIE THE RIBBON THIEF

She led the 1980 women's Boston Marathon from Wellesley to the Pru. At least, she thought she did. "Until I finished," Jacqueline Gareau remembers, "and someone was there in my place."

That someone was Rosie Ruiz, a 26-year-old administrative assistant for a Manhattan precious metals trading firm, who literally came out of nowhere. She had staggered, gasping, across the finish line, then was crowned, medaled and cheered and brought downstairs to sit beside men's victor Bill Rodgers.

"How are you?" he asked Ruiz. "Who are you?"

Nobody had ever seen her finish a marathon before. Nobody saw her run the first 25 miles from Hopkinton. But Ruiz was definitely the first female across the line, in what appeared to be an American record (2 hours 31 minutes 56 seconds), the third-fastest time ever run by a woman. And for a few moments, Ruiz basked in glory.

But it didn't take much longer than a moment for Ruiz to be revealed as a fraud. During the post-race press conference, Ruiz's responses to questions about her training and racing pace sounded ludicrous to seasoned marathoners. She said she'd run only one marathon, turning in a mediocre 2:56:31 in New York. Her fleshy body did not look like that of a serious distance runner.

"Her thighs didn't look in great shape," said then-world-record-holder Derek Clayton. "Her face was not sunken. It's very highly suspect."

Meanwhile, Gareau, who'd finished 2 1/2 minutes behind Ruiz, wandered around the Pru garage in a daze. Gareau was all but certain that Ruiz hadn't been running ahead of her. For the final 13 miles, spectators had told Gareau that she was the lead woman and had informed Patti Lyons, 30 seconds behind her, that she was second.

"Then a mile from the finish, someone called out, 'You're the second woman,' " Gareau remembers. "I thought, 'He must be joking.'"

All the checkpoints along the second half of the race showed Gareau the leader. Soon, the Boston Athletic Association announced it had "grave doubts" about the women's result but wanted to investigate the matter thoroughly.

After a week's investigation the way forward was clear, Ruiz was recorded at no checkpoints. She turned up on no TV film or photograph. The only evidence, other than her breathless sprint at the end, was Ruiz's word. "I came across in 2:31, that's all I have to say," said the woman later described as "troubled" by race organizers..

So the BAA made it official, declaring Gareau the winner in a time of 2:34:26. Ruiz's name and time were scrubbed from the record.

The crown, the medal, all of it came in mid-May, when the BAA brought Gareau down from Quebec for a formal ceremony. They reenacted what should have been, with spectators cheering as Gareau ran across the finish line. "I am probably the only one to cross the finish line in a normal T-shirt and long pants," Gareau remarked. Rodgers held her hand up and said, "I should have done this the first time." ❖

Right: Rosie Ruiz didn't look like a world-class marathon runner, and she didn't sound like a winner at the post-race press conference (far right), either.

BOSTON MARATHON

WHO	**ROSIE RUIZ** VS. **THE RACE MONITORS.**
WHERE	**??? TO BOSTON.**
WHEN	**APRIL 19, 1980.**
WHY THE DRAMA	For 25 miles she wasn't in the race, then suddenly she was the winner. Now she's only the most notorious name in running.

What Happened Next

More trouble

Two years following her moments of infamy in Boston, Rosie Ruiz was arrested in Manhattan on charges of grand larceny and forgery, alleged to have absconded with $15,000 in cash and $45,000 in checks from her employer, a Manhattan real estate firm. She spent a week in jail and was given five years' probation.

Then in November 1983, Ruiz was arrested in Miami for attempting to sell 4.4 pounds of cocaine to undercover narcotics agents. This time she spent 23 days in custody and received two years' probation.

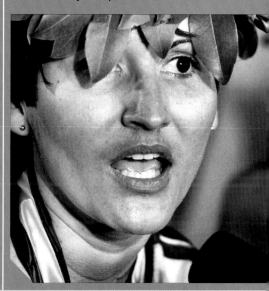

REMEMBERING ROCKY'S HEAVYWEIGHT BELT

The perfect punch was launched in September of 1952 at Municipal Stadium in Philadelphia. When it landed, the Boston sports landscape was forever altered.

On the 23rd of that month, a shoemaker's son from Brockton named Rocco Francis Marchegiano, who was by then known to the rest of the world as Rocky Marciano, threw a short right hand that traveled inches. On impact, it sent a guy appropriately named Arnold Cream to the floor and Marciano to heights no one could have ever predicted.

That one punch not only dethroned Cream, whose fistic alias was Jersey Joe Walcott, but left him a shadow of what he had been. It made Marciano the first New England-born heavyweight champion since Jack Sharkey and the first fighter to win that title while still undefeated since the Boston Strong Boy, John L. Sullivan himself, first won it 70 years earlier.

Earlier, Marciano found himself on the floor for the first time in his career only two minutes into the fight when the normally slow-starting Walcott dropped him with a left hook.

He got up clear-headed, but that was far different from the way he had entered the ring. "My subconscious seemed to take over," Marciano would say of his wandering mind in the fight's initial stages. "Here I was, face to face with my biggest crowd, my biggest purse, and my biggest moment."

And then there he was, face to face with the canvas.

With a reach of only 68 inches (the shortest reach among all heavyweight champs of the 21st century), Marciano had to pay a price to get close enough to extract one from his opponents, but he was blessed with the chin and the heart to do it.

Early in Round 13, Walcott and Marciano launched right hands at the same moment. The champion's back was against the ropes as he fired and Marciano's youthful reflexes were just a hair quicker. His self-proclaimed "Susie Q" smashed into the champion's face right on the jaw, snapping his head around as if it were a broken bobble head doll.

Down Walcott slumped. Referee Charley Daggert counted to 10, but he could have counted to 110. Nothing was going to change. The old man of boxing was taking a nap and no one would awaken him in time to retain his title.

As Walcott snoozed, Marciano kissed his glove while he stood in the neutral corner, savoring the final few seconds of Walcott's reign and the opening moments of his. Much has been written about that punch in the ensuing 50 years, but A.J. Liebling, writing in The New Yorker, offered the clearest and most distinct description of what happened.

"It was, according to old-timers, about as hard as anybody ever hit anybody." Liebling wrote.

In the end, no one else could stand up to Susie Q either, which is why Marciano would retire with a 49-0 record on April 27, 1956, history's only undefeated heavyweight champion. ❖

WORLD HEAVYWEIGHT CHAMPIONSHIP

WHO	**ROCKY MARCIANO** VS. **JERSEY JOE WALCOTT.**
WHERE	**MUNICIPAL STADIUM,** PHILADELPHIA.
WHEN	**SEPTEMBER 23, 1952.**
WHY THE DRAMA	Jersey Joe was the champ. Rocky didn't care.

Hollywood blockbuster vs. Brockton blockbuster

We all know the Rocky Balboa story: Local guy works hard to get his shot at the big time. He's Italian-American, blue collar, puts his family first. He may not be the most skillful man in the ring, but he's got heart. And after he earns our respect in a big-time fight in Philadelphia, he stays true to himself, and loyal to the people that made him.

Pure Hollywood fiction, right? Well, not if you rewind the tale about a quarter century and remove Sylvester Stallone from the picture. Then it becomes the Rocky Marciano story, a real-life triumph by the most famous boxer that Brockton, Massachusetts ever produced.

The epitome of toughness, Marciano (born Rocco Francis Marchegiano in 1923) is often described as having fists of iron and a chin made of steel. He chalked up 42 wins en route to his title shot in Philly.

Jersey Joe Walcott was the champ at the time, but many fans, insiders, and analysts thought he was merely holding the belt until an uncrowned king got his shot. They were thrilled when our underdog Brockton Rocky dug deep and made good, fighting Walcott to a knockout (not a draw, as Stallone's first "Rocky" scripted it) and a championship belt.

When Marciano retired four years and six fights later, he was the only undefeated world heavyweight champion in history. If that had been a movie, no one would have believed it.

A 12TH-ROUND KNOCKOUT

It was a shipwrecker of a punch.

None of us stuffed like galley slaves inside the since-vanished cavern called Boston Garden that 1955 night would ever forget it. The left fist of Tony DeMarco, within a 6-ounce leather glove, gained irresistible momentum as it traveling several blocks up Fleet Street toward the craggy chin of Carmen Basilio.

While paid attendance for that rematch world welterweight championship fight was announced as 9,170, people who knew the leaky building well swore that at least 20,000 were in on it. It felt and sounded as though the populace of DeMarco's motherland, the North End, had relocated to the Garden.

Everybody saw that punch coming, a brother of the left hooks that had shattered Johnny Saxton in the 14th round eight months earlier and transferred the championship from his shoulders to Tony's. Everybody except Basilio, who had taken the title from DeMarco three months after that.

When that punch detonated against Basilio's jaw in the seventh round, the multitude rose screaming, releasing a noise that could have outdone Niagara Falls up close. For an instant the place quaked, seemed to rearrange its foundation and wobble. Basilio, 28, quaked and wobbled, too. His legs were jelly, and an old jazz tune, "It Must Be Jelly 'Cause Jam Don't Shake Like That," skittered through my mind.

"Tony staggered me," Basilio said many years later. "It was a big punch, very big. Everybody wanted me out. That's OK. He was the hometown boy. They were yelling for my blood."

They and DeMarco got some, too, from a gash above Basilio's right eye – but it wasn't enough.

The Basilio ship just wouldn't wreck. As his legs buckled, Basilio clung to whatever part of DeMarco he could. He had to fall, didn't he?

No. Raised on a Canastota, N.Y., farm picking onions, Basilio was somehow rubbing them in the crowd's face, making the loyalists weep. As hope began to clear the cloud in his eyes, he winked one of them at cornerman Angelo Dundee.

Few saw that ocular defiance, though it was clear to some of us in press row. Soon, the local welterweight's chance was slipping away.

First DeMarco, still only 23 that year, was toppled twice in the 10th round. Then he suffered a TKO in the 12th, just as he had in the first fight with Basilio.

Few, if any, Boston athletes have been more an original of The Bean than DeMarco. Born in the Garden's neighborhood at 13 Fleet Street in 1932, he won his world championship within short walking distance. More than 70 years later he lived, comfortably, in an apartment one block from where the Garden stood.

DeMarco's reign as the welterweight champ was brief: 69 days.

"If it had been only one day I would have been happy," DeMarco, who piled up 33 knockouts in 71 starts, said later. "That was my dream, to be a world champion. Looking back, I don't think I gave myself enough rest."

Three title bouts with dangerous adversaries, 38 rounds inside of eight months, was a huge order.

"But I almost got the title back," he said, thinking about the mammoth hook that Basilio absorbed at the Garden. "He should have gone down." ❖

Right: Carmen Basilio wasn't the hometown favorite, but all of Boston had to admire him for standing up to a mammoth punch by Tony DeMarco (far right).

Boxing

WHO	**TONY DEMARCO** VS. **CARMEN BASILIO.**
WHERE	**BOSTON GARDEN.**
WHEN	**JUNE 10, 1955.**
WHY THE DRAMA	The welterweight prince of Boston's North End had the world championship for a few months, lost it, then looked as if he would grab it again.

A champ by any other name

As it turns out, Tony DeMarco wasn't really Tony DeMarco.

Many decades after his final bout, the boxer explained that when he first started fighting he was 16, but he needed to be 18 to get a boxing license.

"I was born Leonardo Liotta and my oldest friends still call me `Nardo,' " he told the Globe. "One of those friends was Tony DeMarco, who was 18. So I borrow his birth certificate. That worked."

Well, for awhile, at least. Until the genuine Tony DeMarco decided to be a boxer.

"He couldn't be DeMarco because I was," recalled our faux DeMarco. "So he borrows the birth certificate of another neighborhood guy, Marco Tremini.

"I'm DeMarco. DeMarco is Tremini, and, luckily, Tremini didn't want to fight."

Got it?

YOU SAY YOU WANT A REVOLUTION? DONE

Near the end of a season filled with memorable rallies, the Revolution put together a comeback that topped them all. They scored three times in a 15-minute span to overcome a one-goal deficit – and a two-goal series deficit – and defeat the New York/New Jersey MetroStars, 3-1, at Gillette Stadium. In so doing, New England earned a spot in the 2005 Major League Soccer conference finals.

Substitutes Jose "Pepe" Cancela and Khano Smith were involved in all the Revolution goals. Cancela scored in the 68th minute and curled a corner kick for Pat Noonan to head in at the 73rd-minute mark, and Smith finished the scoring with a solo run 10 minutes later. In the six times that the Revolution and MetroStars had played each other this season, five of the matches have been decided on goals from the 83d minute on.

"The contributions each of (the reserves) made were huge, said Revolution coach Steve Nicol, "(But) Pepe created the spark when he came on."

The MetroStars won the opener of the total-goal series, 1-0, and extended their series advantage in the 59th minute on Youri Djorkaeff's precise finish of a counterattack.

Six minutes after entering the match in the wake of that score, Cancela advanced on the right side of the penalty area, took a ball chested down by Taylor Twellman, and scored with a low shot. Five minutes later, Noonan nodded one in to give the Revs the lead.

And finally in the 83rd minute, Smith took a pass on the left wing from Clint Dempsey and powered past Eddie Gaven. He proceeded to slam a shot from the edge of the goal area into the far side of the net for a 3-1 lead and a one-goal overall advantage.

The match was played in cold, wet conditions with much of the field covered by a light snowfall. As the field dried in the second half, the Revolution increased their pressure and were able to develop a passing game. The MetroStars were content to counter, which initially paid off in Djorkaeff's goal.

The MetroStars nearly tied up the series again during injury time. Shalrie Joseph cleared a Djorkaeff header off the line, the ball bouncing back to Djorkaeff and just past the right post.

"I knew we wouldn't give up, but I would be lying to you if I said I thought we would win, 3-2, on aggregate," coach Nicol said of the two-goal deficit. "Everyone worked their socks off and we deserved the win." ❖

Left and right: Even bicycle kicks were part of the Revolution's bag of tricks on a day when New England needed to pull out all the stops to score three goals in 15 minutes.

Soccer

MLS CONFERENCE SEMIFINALS

WHO	**REVOLUTION** VS. **METROSTARS.**
WHERE	**GILLETTE STADIUM,** FOXBOROUGH, MASSACHUSETTS.
WHEN	**OCTOBER 29, 2005.**
WHY THE DRAMA	Three goals in 15 minutes doesn't happen every day – especially in soccer.

What Happened Next
Shut out, again

Anyone who'd seen this movie in Foxborough three years prior was familiar with the ending. In the end the camera panned across 11 star-spangled Revs, drained and disheartened, bent over with their hands on their knees after another MLS Cup had been lost. Then it showed 11 exuberant rivals from a Galaxy far, far away jumping into one another's arms.

The scoreboard read Los Angeles 1, New England 0 in overtime – in 2005 just as it was in 2002.

AMATEUR HOUR AT THE US OPEN

In September 1913, Francis Ouimet walked across the street to make history.

The 20-year-old former caddie, who grew up in a modest house on Clyde Street across from The Country Club in Brookline, Massachusetts, had not planned to play in the US Open. But after he won the state amateur that year he was convinced to enter.

The small, select crowd of fans who followed golf had all but conceded the championship to one of the two British professionals who then dominated the game: the legendary Harry Vardon, winner of the US Open in his only previous trip to the United States 13 years earlier, and the long-hitting Ted Ray.

Ouimet, though a pretty good player, was still just a slip of a boy, and an amateur to boot. But as the fourth and final round wound down in steady rain, Ouimet was the only player with a chance. Vardon and Ray were tied for the lead at 304. Ouimet needed a birdie on one of the last two holes, and on No. 17 he hit his approach to 15 feet. Calmly, not distracted by the honking horns coming from the street or the shouts from jubilant spectators, Ouimet sank the curling, down- and side-hill putt for birdie to draw even.

After parring the 18th hole, he was carried off the green on the shoulders of the wildly excited fans, none of whom expected him to come back the next day and beat the British stars in the 18-hole playoff.

But on a sultry, soggy September day, Ouimet vanquished Vardon and Ray by five and six strokes, respectively (72-77-78), setting off the kind of raucous and joyful celebration on the Brookline course not seen again until the 1999 Ryder Cup.

Ouimet was the first amateur to win the US Open. His victory stunned the golf world and enlarged it at the same time, drawing new fans to the sport. Only a quarter of a million people played golf in 1913. Ten years later, it was two million.

He also forever altered the image of golf as a rich man's sport dominated by the British. He was a working-class kid who started caddying when he was 9, toting bags for members of The Country Club for 25 cents a round. He learned to play on a homemade course in the pasture behind his house, sometimes sneaking onto The Country Club's course in the early morning hours. Hole No. 17 was just across the street, and he knew it well. ❖

Top right: Francis Ouimet was barely out of his teens when he and his 10-year-old caddy, Eddie Lowery, stunned the golf world by putting together a US Open win.
Bottom right: Conveniently, the Country Club was practically in Ouimet's backyard.

Golf

WHO	**FRANCIS OUIMET** VS. **HARRY VARDON AND TED RAY.**
WHERE	**THE COUNTRY CLUB,** BROOKLINE, MASSACHUSETTS.
WHEN	**SEPTEMBER 19, 1913.**
WHY THE DRAMA	A decade before there was Bobby Jones there was Francis Ouimet, the first amateur to win a US Open.

Francis Ouimet, who made his living as a stockbroker, twice won the US Amateur championship, in 1914 at Manchester, Vermont, and again in 1931, in Chicago. He played on the US Walker Cup team from 1922, when the series with Britain began, through 1934. He was the non-playing captain from 1936-1949.

He was named an original member of golf's Hall of Fame in 1944, and in 1951 elected captain of the Royal & Ancient Golf Club of St. Andrews, the first non-Briton so honored.

FOUR WINNERS AND A FIRST LADY

he scoreboard operator climbed the small ladder that led to her post, four big 2s in her hand. She inserted them atop the leaderboard, a 22 next to the team of Patty Sheehan and Pat Bradley, and another beside Jan Stephenson and Cindy Rarick.

The pairs of golfers were still tied after four playoff holes and, as the scoreboard showed, they had left par way, way behind. Now with darkness falling and the wind whipping over the hills, something needed to be done to finish the $400,000 BJ's Charity Championship at Granite Links Golf Club in Quincy, Massachusetts. An hour and a half of overtime had not been enough, so the four golfers headed back to the 18th tee once more, and this time they would play from the black championship tees.

But even that was not enough. So after five holes, 10 birdies, and 1 hour 55 minutes in all of extra golf, Sheehan and Bradley and Stephenson and Rarick were declared co-champions of this 2005 Women's Senior Golf Tour Event. It was the tour's first tie in its six-year history.

"This is very, very appropriate," Bradley said before the 200 or so fans who remained. "There shouldn't be a loser in a display of golf like this."

For Bradley, who had journeyed from Westford, Massachusetts to the LPGA and World Golf Halls of Fame, it was yet another amazing finish on the golf course. In her glittering career, the First Lady of New England golf won 31 tournaments and became the first player to capture all four of the LPGA's modern majors — the US Women's Open, the LPGA Championship, the Dinah Shore, and the du Maurier.

Back at the BJ's Charity Championship, after the fourth playoff hole concluded, the four players huddled with course and tour officials to decide how to continue.

All four playoff holes had been tied at birdie on the par-5, 484-yard 18th, which was to be expected considering the scramble format. One idea hatched to finally end play had the players splitting the first-place money, then using a "chip-off" — how that would have worked, we'll never know — to play for the trophy.

"But we're traditionalists," Bradley said.

So instead, they trudged back to the 18th tee again, this time pushing tees into the ground 521 yards from the hole. It was hoped that the extra distance would cause a mistake, open a door. Two birdies later, there were still no losers.

The gallery, worn out from a full day of oohing and aahing, had Bradley mainly to thank for the extended golf. She saved wayward drives and approaches time after time, knocking balls out of bunkers and into safety. After a sand save on the first playoff hole, Rarick turned to the gallery and commented, "How the hell she hits that bunker shot, I'll never know."

Once on the green, Bradley continued to carry Sheehan. Before she made the final putt, Sheehan hadn't putted in two hours. She hadn't needed to.

"I had my pompoms out, just cheering for her," Sheehan said. "She made a mile and a half of putts today. I was like a supporting cast member." ❖

Right: Pat Bradley has seen many exciting finishes in her long and glittering golf career.

Golf

WHO	**PAT BRADLEY, PATTY SHEEHAN, JAN STEPHENSON,** AND **CINDY RARICK**
WHERE	**GRANITE LINKS GOLF CLUB,** QUINCY, MASSACHUSETTS.
WHEN	**AUGUST 7, 2005.**
WHY THE DRAMA	A big-time professional golf tournament can't end in a tie, can it? What about tradition? What about... Gosh, these women just will not stop making birdies.

By-the-book Bradley

Pat Bradley ascended to the top of the golf world in 1986 when she won three of the four majors (just missing a Grand Slam) and was the slam-dunk choice for LPGA Player of the Year. Bradley then had to overcome Graves Disease and eventually became honorary chairman of the Thyroid Foundation of America, establishing a charity pro-am to benefit the organization.

Overall, Bradley won 31 LPGA events including six majors, and was the 12th woman to earn admittance to the LPGA Hall of Fame. She was also a determined defender of the rules of golf. During a second-day four-ball match at the 2000 Solheim Cup in Scotland, Annika Sorenstam pitched in for birdie but did so out of turn, prompting a heated discussion.

Bradley, the American team captain, arrived on the scene and talked to her players, Kelly Robbins and Pat Hurst. Then she did what a team captain should do — took charge — and had Sorenstam play the shot again. Sorenstam didn't make it this time, and Robbins and Hurst went on to halve the match.

Though the European team rolled to an impressive overall victory, Bradley took a lot of heat for her decision. As the Globe's Jim McCabe reported in a later story, her take on the game was simple: "I was just honoring the rules," said Bradley. "There was nothing personal."

OCTOBER 24, 2005 » BY JOHN POWERS, GLOBE STAFF

COLLEGE CREW SURPRISES
HEAD OF THE CHARLES

It was the beginning of the season but the end of the year was in sight, and Princeton's varsity was damned if it was going to let the calendar run out without a major trophy. So the Tigers roared through the final mile at full throttle in the 41st Head of the Charles Regatta and pulled off the biggest upset in race history. They dethroned Cambridge University to win the men's championship eights.

"Hopefully, we've said goodbye to silver and hello to gold," said 7-man Steve Coppola, after his teammates became the first US college crew in 22 years to win the headliner at the world's largest annual two-day regatta by more than 4 seconds over the 3-mile upstream course.

Taken with a triumph by the US national team in the women's race, it marked the first time since 2002 that domestic entries won both championship eights. Persistent Princeton, which hung in gamely despite snapping a steering cable near Weeks Bridge, finished 15 seconds back to claim runners-up honors in that one.

Had the Tigers managed to pull off the men's-women's double, it would have turned the rowing world upside-down. But the men's victory, against a field that included not just Cambridge but world-class boats from Britain, Italy, and the Netherlands, was certainly stunning enough. No American varsity since Navy, which won four in a row ending in 1983, had won the big prize.

When the previous spring season began, Princeton had been favored to win the national collegiate title. But Harvard thwarted the Tigers at every turn, scoring victories in a series of high-profile showdowns.

In the aftermath of those setbacks, Coppola and his teammates resolved to upgrade their precious medals. Even so, gold seemed highly unlikely at the 2005 Head of the Charles.

Princeton believed it had been building toward a statement race ever since Coppola and his classmates arrived on campus three years prior. "These seniors have been the mainstay of the program," coach Curtis Jordan said. "They've never faltered. They keep reaching."

They had to reach against Cambridge, which was first off the line. The Tigers, starting third, never saw the favored Light Blues. They had all they could do to push up on the Dutch while holding off California.

By the time Princeton came around Dead Man's Curve, just before the Eliot Bridge, stroke Sam Loch already had put the hammer down and his seatmates were closing on the Dutch, with coxswain James Egan steering a lovely course. "We always planned that the last mile was when we brought it home," Loch said.

The Tigers did more than that. Between the Cambridge Boat Club and the finish line, less than half a mile, they made up nearly 13 seconds on Cambridge, roughly 3 lengths. The only question: was it enough?

Yes. Princeton (14:41.885) triumphed, Cambridge (14:46.202) was second, and the Dutch team took third. The season of silver was over.

Left: At the John W. Weeks Bridge, the Princeton men's championship eights (far left) had the Dutch boat in their sights.

Rowing

HEAD OF THE CHARLES REGATTA

WHO	**CREW TEAMS FROM AROUND THE WORLD.**
WHERE	**CHARLES RIVER, CAMBRIDGE, MASSACHUSETTS.**
WHEN	**OCTOBER 23, 2005.**
WHY THE DRAMA	No US college had taken top honors at the world's largest regatta in more than 20 years, and Princeton wasn't the one expected to change the status quo.

Always an adventure

Virtually every Head of the Charles brings tales of boats that collide, run aground, and career headlong into abutments. Would it be Boston without the siren song of bumper-thumpers and claims adjusters?

There was the year when a Dartmouth women's eight misjudged the Eliot Street Bridge — the last of numerous not-so-golden arches — and banged bow-first into one of the middle abutments. Another time, the cox of a high school boat panicked, driving his strokers right up on the dock of the Cambridge Boat Club. In '97, three boats charged for the Eliot Bridge, forcing a New York entry to collide with a women's lightweight eight from Tufts. A Keystone Kops pileup ensued, with one woman tossed out of her boat onto an abutment. Unharmed, she scrambled back into her battered barge and the race continued.

There is wind to consider — from the front, side, and back, depending on a boat's location on the course and the meteorology of the moment. There are 90-degree hairpin turns that would challenge supercharged Ferraris, never mind eight-oared slivers of fiberglass, Kevlar, and carbon fiber that stretch nearly 60 feet long. There are even geese, Canadian in origin, brazenly stubborn, and territorial in nature.

At the Head of the Charles, everyone must expect the unexpected. Boats are released from the starting line near the BU boathouse approximately every 15 seconds, but that is usually where any order in the day begins and ends.

"It ain't over till it's over."
—YOGI BERRA

1 final game

THE LITTLE LEAGUE TEAM THAT COULD

There was plenty of plausible justification for their **shortcomings.** They were just kids — "tweens," to use the current terminology — and they were still learning the fundamentals of baseball, let alone executing them. That's what made it so special to watch the feats pulled off by 11- and 12-year-olds from Saugus, Massachusetts at the 2003 Little League World Series.

Their plays often were not clean and crisp. Sometimes they just happened. Sometimes a youngster found himself in the middle of the drama, with no time to do anything except react.

Take Dario Pizzano. His team had just rallied from a three-run deficit against Richmond, Texas, in the seventh inning of the US semifinals to tie a game it had led by six runs an inning earlier. He was at third base, representing the winning run. When teammate Dave Ferreira hit a bouncer between third base and home plate, Pizzano wasn't thinking about proper base running, he was thinking about something far more elemental.

"I was a little nervous that if the third baseman picked it up and threw me out at home, I would have got yelled at," he said.

Pizzano got home so quickly he had time to watch the play at first base — in part because Ferreira hesitated before breaking from the batter's box, thinking the ball was going to roll foul. With a burst of speed, he was called safe at first.

Never mind that Ferreira should not have hesitated, and that replays showed he may have arrived at the base a moment after the catch was made. After all the highs and lows, Saugus prevailed, 14-13, in one of the most thrilling Little League World Series games in history.

"Sure, he should have kept running, but if Dave had kept running, [the play at first] wouldn't have been as close and it wouldn't have been as dramatic," said Saugus manager Rob Rochenski.

He also wanted no part of a discussion over whether Ferreira was safe or out.

"If you're going to question that play, you would have to question the five that came before it," said Rochenski. "It's tough to umpire. They called him safe and he was safe; that's pretty much it."

Before the dramatic rally, several of the youngsters were teary-eyed, but Rochenski, a former Saugus Little Leaguer himself, implored them to save the crying until the contest was over and instead work toward staging a comeback.

Both coaches and players found it difficult to fathom the moment. Before the World Series, Saugus compiled an 18-1 mark. The team posted eight shutouts and scored in double figures 11 times.

They knew the World Series competition would be stiffer, and indeed their first three wins were 2-1, 2-1, and 4-3. When Saugus built a 10-2 lead on Richmond over the first three innings, it appeared to be on the way to the kind of triumph it was more accustomed to.

But Richmond, equally dominant (18-1) before arriving in Williamsport, took Saugus's best shot and countered as no other opponent had. It was more inspiring than any professional game, and tremendous fun to watch. ❖

Right: Saugus's Dave Ferreira was mobbed by his teammates after he hit a single that drove in Dario Pizzano (being hugged in the photo at far right) for the winning run against Richmond in the seventh inning.

Baseball

LITTLE LEAGUE /
WORLD SERIES

WHO	SAUGUS, MASSACHUSETTS VS. RICHMOND, TEXAS
WHERE	WILLIAMSPORT, PENNSYLVANIA
WHEN	AUGUST 21, 2003
WHY THE DRAMA	Imagine you're 12 years old. Imagine the game is on the line. Imagine millions watching your every move. Now imagine you deliver.

	R	H	E
RICHMOND	13	13	2
SAUGUS	14	12	4

What Happened Next

Everyone's a winner

Saugus lost to Boynton Beach, Florida, 9-2, in the US Championship game. Then Boynton Beach lost to Tokyo, 10-1, in the Series final.

No matter.

The boys of Saugus came home to the same kind of heroes' welcome that had greeted 2002 Worcester Little Leaguers after they also finished fourth in the world. This time, the kids were feted at Fenway Park, saluted with a motorcade through their hometown, celebrated on the back of a cereal box, and nominated for an ESPY Award.

At Boston's 2004 victory parade, Laura Lavallee wore a fat lady costume to sing praises of the (at last) World Champion Red Sox.